101 best campsites
for outdoor activities

2013 Edition

alan
rogers

Compiled by: Alan Rogers Guides Ltd

Designed by: Vine Design Ltd

© Alan Rogers Guides Ltd 2012

Published by: Alan Rogers Guides Ltd,
Spelmonden Old Oast, Goudhurst, Kent TN17 1HE

www.alanrogers.com
Tel: 01580 214000

British Library Cataloguing-in-Publication Data:
A catalogue record for this book is available from
the British Library.

ISBN 978-1-906215-94-1

Printed in Great Britain by
Stephens & George Print Group

contents

Welcome to the Alan Rogers
'101' guides

The Alan Rogers guides have been helping campers and caravanners make informed decisions about their holiday destinations since 1968. Today, whether online or in print, Alan Rogers still provides an independent, impartial view, with detailed reports on each campsite.

With so much unfiltered, unqualified information freely available, the Alan Rogers perspective is invaluable to make sure you make the right choice for your holiday.

What is the '101' **series**?

At Alan Rogers, we know that readers have many and diverse interests, hobbies and particular requirements. And we know that our guides, featuring a total of some 3,000 campsites, can provide a bewildering choice from which it can be difficult to produce a shortlist of possible holiday destinations.

The Alan Rogers 101 guides are devised as a means of presenting a realistic, digestible number of great campsites, featured because of their suitability to a given theme.

This book remains first and foremost an authoritative guide to excellent campsites which offer great opportunities to enjoy a range of exciting outdoor activities.

101 **Best campsites for outdoor activities**

Campsites are all about being in the open air, enjoying wonderful natural surroundings. And, of course, time spent on a campsite lends itself to outdoor activities of all sorts, from 'conventional' sports like tennis, to activities often more associated with a holiday, such as kayaking or rafting, through to outward bound pursuits like orienteering and more specialist activities like sand yachting.

Recognising this, campsites have evolved hugely in recent years, investing in new sporting facilities, developing new services and attracting new activity-minded holiday makers.

This is partly due to leisure trends, partly to the influence of organisations like Center Parcs and the Duke of Edinburgh scheme and partly to commercial needs. Many campers are first and foremost activity enthusiasts, for whom staying on a campsite is simply a convenient means of enjoying their chosen activity. Others are 'die-hard' campers who also happen to enjoy a chosen activity.

Alan Rogers – in search of 'the best'

Alan Rogers himself started off with the very specific aim of providing people with the necessary information to allow them to make an informed decision about their holiday destination. Today we still do that with a range of guides that now covers Europe's best campsites in 27 countries.

We work with campsites all day, every day. We visit campsites for inspection purposes (or even just for pleasure!). We know campsites 'inside out'.

We know which campsites would suit active families; which are great for get-away-from-it-all couples; we know which campsites are planning super new pool complexes; which campsites offer a fantastic menu in their on-site restaurant; which campsites allow you to launch a small boat from their slipway; which campsites have a decent playing area for kicking a ball around; which campsites have flat, grassy pitches and which have solid hard standings.

We also know which are good for fishing, golf, spas, children, nature and outdoor activities; which are close to the beach; and which welcome dogs. These particular themes form our '101' series.

All Alan Rogers guides (and our website) are respected for their independent, impartial and honest assessment. The reviews are prose-based, without overuse of indecipherable icons and symbols. Our simple aim is to help guide you to a campsite that matches best your requirements – often quite difficult in today's age of information overload.

What is the **best**?

The criteria we use when inspecting and selecting sites are numerous, but the most important by far is the question of good quality. People want different things from their choice of campsite, so campsite 'styles' vary dramatically: from small peaceful campsites in the heart of the countryside, to 'all singing, all dancing' sites in popular seaside resorts.

The size of the site, whether it's part of a chain or privately owned, makes no difference in terms of it being required to meet our exacting standards in respect of its quality and it being 'fit for purpose'. In other words, irrespective of the size of the site, or the number of facilities it offers, we consider and evaluate the welcome, the pitches, the sanitary facilities, the cleanliness, the general maintenance and even the location.

Expert opinions

We rely on our dedicated team of Site Assessors, all of whom are experienced campers, caravanners or motorcaravanners, to visit and recommend campsites. Each year they travel around Europe inspecting new campsites for Alan Rogers and re-inspecting the existing ones.

When planning
your **holiday**...

A holiday should always be a relaxing affair, and a campsite-based holiday particularly so. Our aim is for you to find the ideal campsite for your holiday, one that suits your requirements. All Alan Rogers guides provide a wealth of information, including some details supplied by campsite owners themselves, and the following points may help ensure that you plan a successful holiday.

Find out more

An Alan Rogers reference number (e.g. FR12345) is given for each campsite and can be useful for finding more information and pictures online at **www.alanrogers.com**
Simply enter this number in the 'Campsite Search' field on the Home page.

Campsite descriptions

We aim to convey an idea of its general appearance, 'feel' and features, with details of pitch numbers, electricity, hardstandings etc.

Facilities

We list specific information on the site's facilities and amenities and, where available, the dates when these facilities are open (if not for the whole season). Much of this information is as supplied to us and may be subject to change. Should any particular activity or aspect of the campsite be important to you, it is always worth discussing with the campsite before you travel.

Swimming pools

Opening dates, any charges and levels of supervision are provided where we have been notified. In some countries (notably France) there is a regulation whereby Bermuda-style shorts may not be worn in swimming pools (for health and hygiene reasons). It is worth ensuring that you do take 'proper' swimming trunks with you.

Charges

Those given are the latest provided to us, usually 2012 prices, and should be viewed as a guide only.

Toilet blocks

We assume that toilet blocks will be equipped with a reasonable number of British style WCs, washbasins and hot showers in cubicles. We also assume that there will be an identified chemical toilet disposal point, and that the campsite will provide water and waste water drainage points and bin areas. If not the case, we comment. We do mention certain features that some readers find important: washbasins in cubicles, facilities for babies, facilities for those with disabilities and motorcaravan service points.

Reservations

Necessary for high season (roughly mid-July to mid-August) in popular holiday areas (i.e. beach resorts). You can reserve many sites via our own Alan Rogers Travel Service or through other tour operators. Remember, many sites are closed all winter and you may struggle to get an answer.

Telephone numbers

All numbers assume that you are phoning from within the country in question. From the UK or Ireland, dial 00, then the country's prefix (e.g. France is 33), then the campsite number given, but dropping the first '0'.

Opening dates

Dates given are those provided to us and can alter before the start of the season. If you intend to visit shortly after a published opening date, or shortly before the closing date, it is wise to check that it will actually be open at the time required. Similarly, some sites operate a restricted service during the low season, only opening some of their facilities (e.g. swimming pools) during the main season; where we know about this, and have the relevant dates, we indicate it – again if you are at all doubtful it is wise to check.

Accommodation

Over recent years, more and more campsites have added high quality mobile homes, chalets, lodges, gites and more. Where applicable we indicate what is available and you'll find details online.

Special Offers

Some campsites have taken the opportunity to highlight a special offer. This is arranged by them and for clarification please contact the campsite direct.

The call of the
great **outdoors**

Campsites across Europe offer a huge range of outdoor activities, and this is the guide to help you find them. You may be a keen mountain biker or windsurfer; you may fancy trying white water rafting or sand yachting during your holiday; or you might simply be looking for a range of exciting activities for the kids this summer (away from the computer screen!).

Either way, there are campsites across Europe offering a chance to enjoy your chosen activity, or try something new. Get out there and give it a try!

Choosing campsites
for outdoor activities

The quality of sporting activities offered by campsites is often remarkable but it's clear that it is no longer enough for a well-run campsite to offer the bare minimum – proper investment, modern infrastructure, quality equipment and qualified professional supervision are all essential.

Convenience and choice

Some campsites offer a wide range of quality activities, aiming for wide appeal to all age groups and interests. This kind of campsite can be a great idea for families with different ages to cater for.

- Camping Ty Nadan in Brittany is exemplary, offering quad biking, aerial zip wires and tree top adventure trails, mountain biking, archery, paintballing and sea kayak excursions.

A specific speciality

Other campsites have become expert in a specific activity, perhaps by virtue of location or personal interest of the owner.

- Camping Wulfener Hals in northern Germany, is ideal for sailing and water sports.

- Camping Jungfrau in Switzerland is ideal for climbing activities.

- Camping Seiser Alm in the Italian Dolomites and Glen Nevis Caravan and Camping Park in Scotland are great bases for mountain pursuits.

Regional specialities

Some people choose their campsite with a particular activity in mind.

- The lakes of the Landes in southwest France offer superb conditions for windsurfing.

- Many waterside campsites in Holland are popular with sailors for their facilities.

for **everyone**

Swimming

Most family campsites these days boast a swimming pool, often an impressive aqua park with slides and pools. But for that 'at one with nature' feel, you can't beat splashing around in a river or lake. Try the tumbling waters of the Ardeche, with pebbly beaches and buzzards wheeling overhead above the craggy cliffs. Or enjoy the cool expanse of inviting waters of a shimmering English lake.

Adventure underground

Some campsites, especially in the Belgian Ardennes, are well placed for underground activities involving caves, potholes, ropes and flashlights.

Up in the trees...

A relatively recent innovation are aerial adventure parks, built up in the treetops of mature woodland. Increasing numbers of campsites have their own (le Ty Nadan in Brittany).

Riding

Some campsites, like Stowford Farm Meadows in Devon, have their own stables and offer riding for all levels. Many others are close to riding facilities.

Canoeing

Canoeing is a great activity on many French campsites, especially in the Ardeche and Dordogne: it's easy to paddle downstream and fun for all the family. Some campsites offer proper tuition, then set you off with lunch in waterproof containers, arranging to meet you downstream and return you to the campsite by minibus.

Watersports

Many campsites are well placed for sailing and windsurfing, some even have their own dinghy launching slipways. Others offer more esoteric activities like kite surfing, scuba diving and water skiing.

Skiing

Skiing is always popular and a little snow should never stop anyone from enjoying a camping holiday! A number of Alpine campsites in France, Austria, and Scandinavia, are open all year round and offer great skiing and snowboarding. Essentials like ski passes and equipment hire are often available while specially adapted mobile homes and accommodation are the norm.

Bikes

Road cycling is hugely popular and easily enjoyed while staying on a campsite. Off road trails for mountain bikes can be found, for example, at Natterersee in the Austrian Tirol.

'Experiences'

Of course, activities can be full-on adrenalin rushes or rather more sedate affairs. A majestic hot air balloon ride over the Loire chateaux, a dawn microlight flight or even an open air painting workshop make for a wonderful and memorable holiday experience.

Outdoor activities for
active **children**

Of course, children enjoy camping holidays at various levels. They enjoy the thrill of sleeping in a different environment; the freedom and fun; and all the small pleasures of being outdoors: pond dipping, watching wildlife, eating breakfast outside every morning. Activities do not always have to be organised.

Children's **Clubs**

Many campsites operate kids' clubs in high season, usually free of charge and multi-national. Activities depend very much on age groups but usually include face painting, treasure hunts, rounders, swimming, circus skills and the like. Activities for older children might include paid-for canoe excursions, bike rides and discos and even rehearsals for a stage show in front of parents at the end of the week.

Qualified instruction…

It's not just the range of activities that is so impressive, it's the degree of professionalism of many campsites. Safety is taken seriously, with appropriate equipment and instruction.

Enjoy…!

Whether you're an 'old hand' or are contemplating your first trip, a regular reader of our Guides or a new 'convert', we wish you well in your travels and hope we have been able to help in some way. We are, of course, also out and about ourselves, visiting sites, talking to owners and readers, and generally checking on standards and new developments. We hope to bump into you!

Wishing you thoroughly enjoyable camping and caravanning in 2013 – favoured by good weather of course!

The Alan Rogers Team

Further **information**

And before you go...

Everyone has different expectations when it comes to holiday activities. And on holiday no-one wants nasty surprises. So be sure to check with the campsite that the activities offered are to your liking before you book.

Insurance

You will naturally have arranged travel insurance for your holiday (and if not, feel free to ask about our own Alan Rogers insurance on 01580 214006 or visit **www.alanrogers.com/travelinsurance**). If planning any dangerous activities please be sure you have appropriate cover.

Camping la Gaviota

Ctra de la Platja s/n, E-17470 Sant Pere Pescador (Girona)
t: **972 520 569** e: **info@lagaviota.com**
alanrogers.com/ES80310 www.lagaviota.com

Accommodation: ☑Pitch ☑Mobile home/chalet ☐Hotel/B&B ☐Apartment

La Gaviota is a delightful, small, family run site at the end of a cul-de-sac with direct beach access. This ensures a peaceful situation with a choice of the pleasant L-shaped pool or the fine clean beach with slowly shelving access to the water. Everything here is clean and smart and the Gil family are very keen that you enjoy your time here. There are 165 touring pitches on flat ground with shade and 8A electricity supply. A lush green feel is given to the site by many palms and other semi-tropical trees and shrubs. The restaurant and bar are very pleasant indeed and have a distinct Spanish flavour. The cuisine is reasonably priced, perfectly prepared and served by friendly staff. All facilities are at the reception end of this rectangular site with extra washing up areas at the far end. The guests here were happy and enjoying themselves when we visited. English is spoken.

You might like to know
Sant Pere Pescador is an outstanding destination for windsurfers and kite surfers thanks to the Tramuntana and Garbi winds.

- ☑ Riding
- ☑ Tennis
- ☑ Cycling *(road)*
- ☑ Outdoor pool
- ☑ Crafts
- ☑ Sailing
- ☑ Windsurfing
- ☑ Kitesurfing
- ☑ Diving
- ☑ Golf
- ☑ Kayaking
- ☑ Go-karting
- ☑ Fishing

Facilities: One smart and very clean toilet block is near reception. All WCs are British style and the showers are excellent. Superb facilities for disabled visitors. Two great family rooms plus two baby rooms. Washing machine. Gas supplies. Supermarket (fresh bread), pleasant bar and small, delightful restaurant (all Mar-Oct). Swimming pool (May-Oct). Playground. Games room. Limited animation. Beach sports and windsurfing. WiFi over site (charged). Torches useful. ATM. Off site: Boat launching 2 km. Riding 4 km. Sailing 10 km. Golf 15 km. Boat excursions. Cycling routes.

Open: 23 March - 28 October.

Directions: From the AP7/E15 take exit 3 onto the N11 north towards Figueras and then the C260 towards Roses. At Castello d'Empúries take the GIV 6216 and continue to Sant Pere Pescador. Site is well signed in the town. GPS: 42.18901, 3.10843

Charges guide

Per unit incl. 2 persons and electricity	€ 23,95 - € 51,95
extra person	€ 3,50 - € 4,50
child (under 10 yrs)	€ 1,50 - € 3,00
dog	€ 2,00 - € 4,00

No credit cards.

Camping Las Palmeras

Ctra de la Platja, E-17470 Sant Pere Pescador (Girona)
t: **972 520 506** e: **info@campinglaspalmeras.com**
alanrogers.com/ES80330 www.campinglaspalmeras.com

Accommodation: ☑Pitch ☑Mobile home/chalet ☐Hotel/B&B ☐Apartment

A very polished site, the pleasant experience begins as you enter the palm bedecked site and are welcomed at the airy reception building. The 230 pitches are flat, very clean and well maintained, with some shade and 10A electricity. A few pitches are complete with water and drainage. Thirty smart mobile homes are placed unobtrusively around the site. A very pleasant pool complex has a lifeguard and the brightly coloured play areas are clean and safe. A great beach is just a 200 m. walk through a gate at the rear of the site. A full activities programme for children allows parents a break during the day and there is organised fun in the evenings in high season. Full recreational facilities include a gym. The very Spanish style restaurant serves high quality food. The owner, Juan Carlos Alcantara, and his wife have years of experience in the campsite business, which is clearly demonstrated. You will enjoy your stay here as there is a very happy atmosphere.

You might like to know

Las Palmeras is adjacent to the Punta de la Mora natural park, a great area for walking and cycling.

- ☑ Riding
- ☑ Tennis
- ☑ Cycling *(road)*
- ☑ Outdoor pool
- ☑ Crafts
- ☑ Sailing
- ☑ Windsurfing
- ☑ Kitesurfing
- ☑ Diving
- ☑ Waterskiing

- ☑ Golf
- ☑ Paintball
- ☑ Hiking
- ☑ Fitness/gym
- ☑ Go-karting

Facilities: Two excellent, very clean, solar powered toilet blocks include first class facilities for disabled campers. Baby rooms. Facilities may become a little busy at peak periods. Washing machines. Motorcaravan services. Supermarket, restaurant/bar/takeaway open all season (children's menu). Swimming pools (heated). Play areas. Tennis. Five-a-side. Fronton. Boules. Gym. Barbecue. Bicycle hire. Miniclub. Entertainment. Satellite TV. Internet access. WiFi throughout (charged). ATM. Torches useful. Off site: Beach and fishing 200 m. Sailing and boat launching 2 km. Riding 4 km. Golf 7 km.

Open: 31 March - 20 October.

Directions: Sant Pere Pescador is south of Perpignan on coast between Roses and L'Escala. From the AP7/E15 take exit 4 north on N11 towards Figueres and then C31 towards Torroella de Fluvia. Take the Vilamacolum road east and continue to Sant Pere Pescador. Site well signed in town. GPS: 42.18805, 3.1027

Charges guide

Per unit incl. 2 persons and electricity	€ 24,30 - € 52,90
extra person	€ 3,20 - € 4,60
child (2-9 yrs)	€ 1,70 - € 2,80

No credit cards.

Camping Las Dunas

Ctra San Marti-Sant Pere, E-17470 Sant Pere Pescador (Girona)
t: **972 521 717** e: **info@campinglasdunas.com**
alanrogers.com/ES80400 www.campinglasdunas.com

Accommodation: ☑Pitch ☑Mobile home/chalet ☐ Hotel/B&B ☐Apartment

Las Dunas is an extremely large, impressive and well organised resort style site with many on-site activities and an ongoing programme of improvements. It has direct access to a superb sandy beach that stretches along the site for nearly a kilometre with a windsurfing school and beach bar. There is also a much used, huge swimming pool, plus a large double pool for children. Las Dunas is very large, with 1,700 individual hedged pitches (1,500 for touring units) of around 100 sq.m. laid out on flat ground in long, regular parallel rows. All have electricity (6/10A) and 180 also have water and drainage. Shade is available in some parts of the site. Pitches are usually available, even in the main season. Much effort has gone into planting palms and new trees here and the results are very attractive. The large restaurant and bar have spacious terraces overlooking the swimming pools or you can enjoy a very pleasant, more secluded, cavern style pub. A magnificent disco club is close by in a soundproofed building (although people returning from this during the night can be a problem for pitches in the central area of the site). A member of Leading Campings Group.

You might like to know
Las Dunas offers sports competitions, games and other activities organised by a team of professional entertainers.

- ☑ Riding
- ☑ Tennis
- ☑ Cycling (road)
- ☑ Cycling (mountain biking)
- ☑ Sports field
- ☑ Outdoor pool
- ☑ Crafts
- ☑ Archery
- ☑ Sailing
- ☑ Windsurfing

- ☑ Kitesurfing
- ☑ Diving
- ☑ Waterskiing
- ☑ Hiking
- ☑ Kayaking

Facilities: Five excellent large toilet blocks with electronic sliding glass doors (resident cleaners 07.00-21.00). British style toilets but no seats, controllable hot showers and washbasins in cabins. Excellent facilities for youngsters, babies and disabled campers. Laundry facilities. Motorcaravan services. Extensive supermarket, boutique and other shops. Large bar with terrace. Large restaurant. New takeaway and terrace in 2012. Ice cream parlour. Beach bar in main season. Disco club. Swimming pools. Playgrounds. Tennis. Archery. Minigolf. Sailing/windsurfing school and other watersports. Programme of sports, games, excursions and entertainment, partly in English (15/6-31/8). Exchange facilities. ATM. Safety deposit. Internet café. WiFi over site (charged). Dogs taken in one section. Torches required in some areas.

Open: 18 May - 14 September.

Directions: L'Escala is northeast of Girona on the coast between Palamós and Roses. From A7/E15 autostrada take exit 5 towards L'Escala on GI623. Turn north 2 km. before reaching L'Escala towards Sant Marti d'Ampúrias. Site well signed. GPS: 42.16098, 3.13478

Charges guide

Per unit incl. 2 persons and electricity	€ 22,50 - € 68,00

Camping Internacional de Calonge

Ctra San Feliu/Guixols - Palamós km 7.6, E-17251 Calonge (Girona)
t: 972 651 233 e: info@intercalonge.com
alanrogers.com/ES81300 www.intercalonge.com

Accommodation: ☑Pitch ☑Mobile home/chalet ☐ Hotel/B&B ☐ Apartment

This spacious, well laid out site has access to a fine beach via a footbridge over the coast road, or you can take the little road train as the site is on very sloping ground. Calonge is a family site with two good sized pools on different levels, a paddling pool and large sunbathing areas. A great restaurant, bar and snack bar are by the pool. The site's 793 pitches are on terraces and all have electricity (5A), with 84 being fully serviced. The pitches are set on attractively landscaped terraces (access to some may be challenging). There is good shade from the tall pine trees, and some views of the sea through the foliage. The views from the upper levels are taken by a tour operator and mobile home pitches. The pools are overlooked by the restaurant terraces which have great views over the mountains. A nature area within the site is used for walks and picnics. A separate area within the site is set aside for visitors with dogs (including a dog shower!). The beach is accessed over the main road by 100 steps and is shared with another campsite (ES81400).

You might like to know

A special weekly programme is available in collaboration with Tennis World at Platja d'Aro, including friendship games with club members.

- ☑ Riding
- ☑ Pony trekking
- ☑ Tennis
- ☑ Cycling (road)
- ☑ Cycling (mountain biking)
- ☑ Sports field
- ☑ Outdoor pool
- ☑ Crafts
- ☑ Sailing
- ☑ Surfing

- ☑ Windsurfing
- ☑ Diving
- ☑ Golf
- ☑ Hiking
- ☑ Kayaking

Facilities: Generous sanitary provision in new and renovated blocks include some washbasins in cabins. No toilet seats. One block is heated in winter. Laundry facilities. Motorcaravan services. Gas supplies. Shop (26/3-30/10). Restaurant (1/2-31/12). Bar, patio bar with pizzas and takeaway (27/3-24/10, weekends for the rest of the year). Swimming pools (26/3-16/10). Playground. Electronic games. Rather noisy disco two nights a week (but not late). Bicycle hire. Tennis. Hairdresser. ATM. Internet access and WiFi. Torches necessary in some areas. Road train from the bottom of the site to the top in high season. Off site: Bus at the gate. Fishing 300 m. Supermarket 500 m. Golf 3 km. Riding 10 km.

Open: All year.

Directions: Site is on inland side of the coast road between Palamós and Platja d'Aro. Take C31 south to 661 at Calonge. At Calonge follow signs to C253 towards Platja d'Aro and on to site which is well signed. GPS: 41.83333, 3.08417

Charges guide

Per unit incl. 2 persons and electricity	€ 20,25 - € 47,70
extra person	€ 3,70 - € 8,35
child (3-10 yrs)	€ 1,85 - € 4,55

No credit cards.

Camping Picos de Europa

E-33556 Avin-Onis (Asturias)
t: 985 844 070   e: info@picos-europa.com
alanrogers.com/ES89650   www.picos-europa.com

Accommodation: ☑Pitch ☑Mobile home/chalet ☐ Hotel/B&B ☑Apartment

This delightful site is, as its name suggests, an ideal spot from which to explore these dramatic limestone mountains on foot, by bicycle or on horseback. The site itself is continuously developing and the dynamic owner, José, and his nephew who helps out when he is away, are both very pleasant and nothing is too much trouble. The site is in a valley beside a pleasant, fast flowing river. The 160 marked pitches are of varying sizes and have been developed in three avenues, on level grass mostly backing on to hedging, with 6A electricity. An area for tents and apartments is over a bridge past the fairly small, but pleasant, round swimming pool. Local stone has been used for the L-shaped building at the main entrance which houses reception and a very good bar/restaurant. The site can organise caving activities, and has information about the Cares gorge along with the many energetic ways of exploring the area, including by canoe and quad-bike! The Bulnes funicular railway is well worth a visit.

You might like to know

White-water canoeing at the Sella descent has different starting points, providing courses from 6 km. to 14 km. One- two- and three-seat canoes are available.

- ☑ Riding
- ☑ Cycling *(mountain biking)*
- ☑ Outdoor pool
- ☑ Rafting
- ☑ Canyoning
- ☑ Potholing
- ☑ Hiking
- ☑ Aerial walkways
- ☑ Canoeing
- ☑ Kayaking

Facilities: Toilet facilities include a new fully equipped block, along with new facilities for disabled visitors and babies. Pleasant room with tables and chairs for poor weather. Washing machine and dryer. Shop (July-Sept). Swimming pool (Feb-Sept). Bar and cafeteria style restaurant (all year) serves a good value 'menu del dia' and snacks. WiFi in restaurant area. Play area. Fishing. Torches necessary in the new tent area. Off site: Riding 12 km. Bicycle hire 15 km. Golf and coast at Llanes 25 km.

Open: All year.

Directions: Avln is 15 km. east of Cangas de On's on AS114 to Panes and is best approached from this direction especially if towing. From A8 (Santander-Oviedo) km. 326 exit take N634 northwest to Arriondas. Turn southeast on N625 to Cangas and join AS114 (Covodonga/Panes) bypassing Cangas. Site is beyond Avln after 16 km. marker. GPS: 43.3363, -4.94498

Charges guide

Per person	€ 5,02
child (under 14 yrs)	€ 4,01
pitch incl. car	€ 8,57 - € 9,64
electricity	€ 3,75

Marjal Camping & Bungalows Resort

Ctra N332 km. 73,4, E-03140 Guardamar del Segura (Alacant)
t: **966 727 070** e: **camping@marjal.com**
alanrogers.com/ES87430 www.campingmarjal.com

Accommodation: ☑Pitch ☑Mobile home/chalet ☐Hotel/B&B ☐Apartment

Marjal is located beside the estuary of the Segura river, alongside the pine and eucalyptus forests of the Dunas de Guardamar Natural Park. A fine sandy beach can be reached through the forest (800 m). This is a very smart site with a huge tropical lake-style pool with bar and a superb sports complex. There are 212 pitches on this award-winning site, 168 for touring with water, electricity (16A), drainage and satellite TV points. The ground is covered with crushed marble, making the pitches clean and pleasant. There is some shade and the site has an open feel with lots of room for manoeuvring. Reception is housed within a delicately coloured building complete with a towering Mirador, topped by a weather vane depicting the 'garza real' (heron) bird which frequents the local area and forms part of the site logo. The large restaurant overlooks the pools and the river that leads to the sea in the near distance. The bar has large terraces fringed by trees, palms and pomegranates. The impressive pool/lagoon complex (1,100 sq.m) has a water cascade, an island bar plus bridge, one part sectioned as a pool for children and a jacuzzi.

You might like to know

Why not take a day trip to Guardamar del Segura, a typical Spanish town which has excellent beaches, a thriving street market and a variety of shops, bars and restaurants?

- ☑ Riding
- ☑ Tennis
- ☑ Sports field
- ☑ Outdoor pool
- ☑ Golf
- ☑ Fitness/gym
- ☑ Aerobics
- ☑ Aquarobics
- ☑ Minigolf

Facilities: Three excellent heated toilet blocks have free hot water, elegant separators between sinks, spacious showers and some cabins. Each block has high quality facilities for babies and disabled campers, modern laundry and dishwashing rooms. Motorcaravan service point. Car wash. Well stocked supermarket. Restaurants. Bar. Large outdoor pool complex (1/6-31/10). Heated indoor pool (low season). Jacuzzi. Sauna. Solarium. Beauty salon. Superb well equipped gym. Aerobics. Physiotherapy. All activities discounted for campers. Play room. Minigolf. Floodlit tennis and soccer pitch. Bicycle hire. Car rental. Games room. TV room. Full entertainment programme. Hairdresser. ATM. Business centre. Internet access and free WiFi over site. Caravan storage. Off site: Beach 800 m. Fishing 1 km. Riding and golf 4 km.

Open: All year.

Directions: On N332 40 km. south of Alicante, site is on the sea side between 73 and 74 km. markers. GPS: 38.10933, -0.65467

Charges guide

Per unit incl. 2 persons and electricity	€ 38,00 - € 65,00
extra person	€ 7,00 - € 9,00
child (4-12 yrs)	€ 5,00 - € 6,00

Orbitur Camping Rio Alto

EN13 km. 13 Rio Alto-Est, Estela, P-4570-275 Póvoa de Varzim (Porto)
t: **252 615 699**   e: **inforioalto@orbitur.pt**
alanrogers.com/PO8030   www.orbitur.pt

Accommodation: ☑Pitch ☑Mobile home/chalet   ☐ Hotel/B&B   ☐Apartment

This site makes an excellent base for visiting Porto which is some 35 km. south of
Estela. It has around 700 pitches on sandy terrain and is next to what is virtually
a private beach. There are some hardstandings for caravans and motorcaravans and
electrical connections to most pitches (long leads may be required). The area for tents
is furthest from the beach and windswept, stunted pines give some shade. There
are arrangements for car parking away from camping areas in peak season. There is
a quality restaurant, a snack bar and a large swimming pool across the road from
reception. An 18-hole golf course is adjacent and huge nets along one side of the site
protect campers from any stray balls. The beach is accessed via a novel double tunnel
in two lengths of 40 metres beneath the dunes (open 09.00-19.00). The beach shelves
steeply at some tidal stages (lifeguard 15/6-15/9).

You might like to know

The first European campsite to be certified for
service quality standards by SGS ICS. Rio Alto
has direct access to a fine beach, via a tunnel
beneath a golf course in the heart of
Portugal's Green Coast.

☑ **Riding**
☑ **Tennis**
☑ **Cycling** (road)
☑ **Sports field**
☑ **Outdoor pool**
☑ **Sailing**
☑ **Windsurfing**
☑ **Golf**
☑ **Kayaking**
☑ **Fishing**

Facilities: Four refurbished and well equipped
toilet blocks have hot water. Laundry facilities.
Facilities for disabled visitors. Gas supplies.
Motorcaravan service point. Shop. Restaurant,
bar, snack bar (1/5-31/10). Swimming pool
(1/6-30/9). Tennis. Playground. Games room.
Surfing. TV. Medical post. Car wash. Evening
entertainment twice weekly in season. Bicycle
hire can be arranged by reception. WiFi.
Off site: Fishing. Golf. Riding (all within 5 km).

Open: All year.

Directions: From A28 in direction of Porto, leave
at exit 18 signed Fao/Apuila. At roundabout take
third exit, N13 in direction of Pavoa de Varzim for
2.5 km. At Hotel Contriz, turn right onto narrow
cobbled road. Site well signed in 2 km.
GPS: 41.44504, -8.75767

Charges guide

Per unit incl. 2 persons and electricity	€ 19,10 - € 33,60
extra person	€ 3,70 - € 6,10
child (5-10 yrs)	€ 1,90 - € 3,10
dog	€ 1,00 - € 2,00

PORTUGAL – Odemira
Zmar-Eco Camping Resort

Herdade A de Mateus EN393/1, San Salvador, P-7630 Odemira (Beja)
t: 707 200 626 e: info@zmar.eu
alanrogers.com/PO8175 www.zmar.eu

Accommodation: ☑Pitch ☑Mobile home/chalet ☐Hotel/B&B ☐Apartment

Zmar is an exciting new project which should be fully open this year. The site is located near Zambujeira do Mar, on the Alentejo coast. This is a highly ambitious initiative developed along very strict environmental lines. For example, renewable resources such as locally harvested timber and recycled plastic are used wherever possible and solar energy is used whenever practicable. Public indoor spaces have no air conditioning, but there is adequate cooling through underfloor ventilation and electric fans where possible. Pitches are 100 sq.m. and benefit from artificial shade. Caravans and wood-clad mobile homes are also available for rent. The swimming pool complex features a large outdoor pool and an indoor pool area with a wave machine and a wellness centre. The very large and innovative children's play park has climbing nets, labyrinths and caves. There is also a children's farm and a large play house. For adults, many sporting amenities will be available around the resort's 81-hectare park. These will include a sports field, bicycle hire, tennis courts under a huge tent and a military-style climbing and abseiling adventure installation.

You might like to know
On the campsite you will find a Centre for Environmental Interpretation describing the fauna, flora and climate of the region, and displaying a selection of historical artefacts.

☑ Tennis
☑ Cycling *(mountain biking)*
☑ Sports field
☑ Outdoor pool
☑ Archery
☑ Hiking
☑ Canoeing
☑ Fitness/gym
☑ Fishing
☑ Treetop Adventures

Facilities: Eight toilet blocks provide comprehensive facilities, including those for children and disabled visitors. Bar. Restaurant. Crêperie. Takeaway. Large supermarket. Swimming pool. Covered pool. Wellness centre. Sports field. Games room. Play area, farm and play house. Tennis. Bicycle hire. Activity and entertainment programme. Mobile homes and caravans for rent. Caravan repair and servicing. The site's own debit card system is used for payment at all facilities. Off site: Vicentina coast and the Alentejo Natural Park. Sines (birthplace of Vasco de Gama). Cycle and walking tracks. Sea fishing.

Open: All year.

Directions: From the N120 from Odemira to Lagos, at roundabout in the centre of Portas de Transval turn towards Milfontes. Take turn to Cabo Sardo and then Zambujeira do Mar. Site is on the left. GPS: 37.60422, -8.73142

Charges guide

Per unit incl. up to 4 persons and electricity	€ 20,00 - € 50,00
extra person	€ 5,00 - € 10,00
child (4-12 yrs)	€ 5,00

ITALY – Caorle

Centro Vacanze Pra' Delle Torri

P.O. Box 176, via Altanea 201, I-30021 Caorle (Veneto)
t: **042 129 9063** e: **info@pradelletorri.it**
alanrogers.com/IT60030 www.pradelletorri.it

Accommodation: ☑Pitch ☑Mobile home/chalet ☑Hotel/B&B ☐Apartment

Pra' Delle Torri is a superb Italian Adriatic site which has just about everything! Pitches for camping, hotel, accommodation to rent and two very large, well equipped pool complexes, which may be rated among the best in the country. There is also a full size golf course. Of the 1,500 pitches, 888 are available for touring and are arranged in zones, with 5-10A electricity and shade. There is an amazing choice of good restaurants, bars and shops arranged around an attractive square. Although a large site, there is a great atmosphere here that families will enjoy.The fabulous lagoon pool complex with islands, slides and sunbathing areas is the site's crowning glory, plus indoor (Olympic size) and outdoor lane pools. Other super amenities include a large grass area for ball games, a good playground, a children's car track, and a whole range of sports, fitness and entertainment programmes, along with a medical centre, skin care and other therapies. The site has its own sandy beach and Porto, Santa Margherita and Caorle are nearby. One could spend a whole holiday here without leaving the site but the attractions of Venice, Verona, etc. might well tempt one to explore the area.

You might like to know
A few steps away is the enchanting maritime town of Caorle, with typical restaurants, and just along the coast is Venice, with its thousand-year-old history.

- ☑ Riding
- ☑ Tennis
- ☑ Cycling (mountain biking)
- ☑ Outdoor pool
- ☑ Archery
- ☑ Diving
- ☑ Golf
- ☑ Fitness/gym
- ☑ 10-pin bowling
- ☑ Fishing

Facilities: Sixteen high quality toilet blocks with excellent facilities including very attractive 'junior stations'. Units for disabled visitors. Laundry facilities. Motorcaravan service point. Large supermarket and wide range of shops, restaurants, bars and takeaways. Indoor and outdoor pools. Tennis. Minigolf. Fishing. Watersports. Archery. Diving. Fitness programmes and keep fit track. Crèche and supervised play area. Bowls. Mountain bike track. Wide range of organised sports and entertainment. Road train to town in high season. Dogs are not accepted. Off site: Riding 3 km. Beach fishing. Tours and excursions.

Open: 21 April - 30 September.

Directions: From A4 Venice-Trieste motorway leave at exit for Santo Stino di Livenze and follow signs to Caorle then Santa Margherita and signs to site. GPS: 45.57312, 12.81248

Charges guide

Per unit incl. 2 persons and electricity	€ 16,40 - € 62,80
extra person	€ 4,20 - € 9,90
child (2-5 yrs)	free - € 7,00
child (6-12 yrs)	€ 1,00 - € 8,20

Min. stay 2 nights.

ITALY – Cavallino-Treporti

Camping Union Lido Vacanze

Via Fausta 258, I-30013 Cavallino-Treporti (Veneto)
t: 041 257 5111 e: info@unionlido.com
alanrogers.com/IT60200 www.unionlido.com

Accommodation: ☑Pitch ☑Mobile home/chalet ☐Hotel/B&B ☐Apartment

This amazing site is very large, offering everything a camper could wish for. It is extremely well organised and it has been said to set the standard that others follow. It lies right beside the sea with direct access to a 1.2 km. long, broad sandy beach which shelves very gradually and provides very safe bathing (there are lifeguards). The site itself is regularly laid out with parallel access roads under a covering of poplars, pine and other trees providing good shade. There are 2,222 pitches for touring units, all with 6/10A electricity and 1,777 also have water and drainage. Because of the size of the site, there is an internal road train and amenities are repeated across the site (cycling is not permitted and cars are parked away from the pitches). You really would not need to leave this site – everything is here, including a sophisticated wellness centre. Overnight parking is provided outside the gate with electricity, toilets and showers for those arriving after 21.00. There are two aqua parks, one with fine sandy beaches (a first in Europe) and both with swimming pools, lagoon pools for children, a heated whirlpool and a slow flowing 160 m. 'river'. A member of Leading Campings group.

You might like to know

An exclusive 15-acre natural wood area near the beach for jogging, children's games and a signed nature itinerary. We also offer aqua gym, windsurf, swimming school and beach volleyball programmes.

☑ Riding
☑ Pony trekking
☑ Tennis
☑ Sports field
☑ Outdoor pool
☑ Surfing
☑ Diving
☑ Golf
☑ Fitness/gym

Facilities: Fourteen well kept, fully equipped toilet blocks; 11 have facilities for disabled visitors. Launderette. Motorcaravan service points. Gas supplies. Comprehensive shopping areas set around a pleasant piazza (all open until late). Eight restaurants plus 11 pleasant and lively bars (all services open all season). Impressive aqua parks (all season). Tennis. Riding. Minigolf. Skating. Bicycle hire. Archery. Two fitness tracks in 4 ha. natural park with play area and supervised play for children. Golf academy. Diving centre and school. Windsurfing school in season. Boat excursions. Recreational events. Hairdressers. Internet cafés. ATM. Dogs are not accepted. WiFi throughout (charged). Off site: Boat launching 3.5 km. Aqualandia.

Open: 21 April - 23 September (with all services).

Directions: From Venice-Trieste autostrada leave at exit for airport or Quarto d'Altino and follow signs first for Jesolo and then Punta Sabbioni, and site will be seen just after Cavallino on the left. GPS: 45.467883, 12.530367

Charges guide

Per unit incl. 2 persons and electricity	€ 25,40 - € 48,60
with services	€ 28,50 - € 65,60
extra person	€ 6,60 - € 11,45

ITALY – Lido di Jesolo

Camping Jesolo International

Viale A. da Giussano, I-30016 Lido di Jesolo (Veneto)
t: **042 197 1826** e: **info@jesolointernational.it**
alanrogers.com/IT60370 www.jesolointernational.it

Accommodation: ☑Pitch ☑Mobile home/chalet ☐ Hotel/B&B ☐Apartment

At this brilliant family resort-style site with a focus on sporting activities, you can plan the cost of your holiday with confidence. The amazing array of on-site activities is included in the price and there are large discounts for some off-site attractions. Jesolo International is located on a beautiful promontory with 700 m. of uncrowded white sandy beach and slowly shelving waters for safe swimming. As the site is narrow, all the pitches are close to the sea. There is a choice of two types of pitch, all flat, well shaded and with 10/20A electricity, water and drainage, WiFi and satellite TV connection. Each 'ultra' pitch has a private bathroom. Chalet accommodation is excellent. This is said to be the first carbon neutral campsite in the world. The superb pool complex, where an excellent entertainment programme is presented each night, is centrally located and very spacious. The dynamic director Sergio Comino works long hours to maintain and improve this high quality, family orientated site, to combine a unique holiday experience for guests, with real value for money.

You might like to know
It is an exemplary environmental concept, the only 'CO² neutral' campsite in Europe.

- ☑ Riding
- ☑ Tennis
- ☑ Outdoor pool
- ☑ Archery
- ☑ Sailing
- ☑ Diving
- ☑ Golf
- ☑ Pedaloes
- ☑ Fitness/gym
- ☑ Go-karting

Facilities: Sanitary facilities include 72 modern, continually cleaned bathroom units and baby rooms. Washing machines and dryers. Dishwashers. Motorcaravan service point. Supermarket. Family style restaurant. Beach bar with snacks. Pool bar serving light lunches. Sports centre. Children's club. Indoor gym. Tennis courts (free use and lessons). Golf (lessons and fees all free). Sailing with tuition. Large grassy play area with adventure style equipment. WiFi free. Banana boat, canoes, pedal boats, loungers and sunshades (all free). Doctor on site (free). Scuba diving (free; introductory lesson). Language course (free). Pony riding (free). Pirates ship (free). Dogs are not accepted. Off site: Ferry to Venice and Murano 200 m. Jesolo promenade with shops, restaurants and bars 500 m. Aqualandia 1.5 km.

Open: 28 April - 30 September.

Directions: From A4 Venice-Trieste autostrada take Dona di Piave exit and follow signs to Jesolo then Punta Sabbioni. Turn off to Lido di Jesolo just before the Cavallino bridge where the site is well signed. GPS: 45.48395, 12.58763

Charges guide

Per unit incl. 2 persons and electricity	€ 27,50 - € 57,00
extra person	€ 6,00 - € 13,50

ITALY – Lana

Naturcaravanpark Tisens

I-39010 Tisens (Trentino - Alto Adige)
t: 0473 927 131   e: info@naturcaravanpark-tisens.com
alanrogers.com/IT61844   www.naturcaravanpark-tisens.com

Accommodation: ☑Pitch ☐ Mobile home/chalet ☐ Hotel/B&B ☐Apartment

Naturcaravanpark Tisens is a new site, open all year and located amidst orchards in tranquil Alpine surroundings. It can be found 10 minutes walk from the centre of Tesimo (Tisens) and midway between Merano and Bolzano (both 14 km. distant). Pitches here are of a good size (around 90 sq.m). A number of larger pitches and 'panoramic' pitches (120 sq.m) are also available. Each pitch has 6A electricity, water and drainage. The impressive toilet block is brand new and heated. A small shop is well stocked with essential supplies. The site's 25 m. heated swimming pool and the smaller children's pool (also heated) are surounded by meadows, ideal for sunbathing, with fine mountain views on all sides. Off site, there are miles of excellent walking and cycle tracks close at hand, and bicycle hire is available on site. The village of Tisens (Tesimo) is located on a plateau 650 m. above sea level. This is a peaceful spot, surrounded by chestnut groves and some of Europe's most ancient vineyards.

You might like to know
This new site is located in open countryside amidst orchards, just ten minutes' walk from Tesimo town centre and 7 km. from Lana.

- ☑ Horse riding
- ☑ Tennis
- ☑ Cycling (mountain biking)
- ☑ Sports field
- ☑ Outdoor pool
- ☑ Golf
- ☑ Rock climbing
- ☑ Hiking

Facilities: Impressive new, heated toilet block, Shop. Café/snack bar. Swimming pool. Children's pool. Bicycle hire. Playground. Tourist information. Off site: Walking and cycling. Tennis. Golf. Riding. Merano and Bolzano 14 km.

Open: All year.

Directions: Approaching from the A22 motorway and Brenner Pass, take the Merano Sud exit and follow signs to Lana. From there head towards Palade/Gampenpass as far as Tesimo/Tisens, from where the site is well signed.
GPS: 46.56218, 11.17608

Charges guide

Per unit incl. 2 persons, electricity, water and drain	€ 27,00 - € 32,00
extra person	€ 6,00
child (5-10 yrs)	€ 3,50
dog	free

ITALY – Sarnonico-Fondo

Camping Park Baita Dolomiti

Via Cesare Battisti 18, I-38010 Sarnonico-Fondo (Trentino - Alto Adige)
t: **046 383 0109** e: **campark@tin.it**
alanrogers.com/IT61980 **www.baita-dolomiti.it**

Accommodation: ☑Pitch ☑Mobile home/chalet ☐Hotel/B&B ☐Apartment

Baita Dolomiti is a family campsite located in a splendid mountain region. It was very quiet when we visited in early June, but apparently becomes quite lively in high season, with plenty of organised entertainment for young and old. There is a rustic bar and restaurant providing typical local meals. The 130 grass touring pitches all have 3A electricity and, although they are not large, there is a great sense of space. The Val di Non is a wonderful area for walking and cycling and the more adventurous can explore the canyons on foot or by boat. The Dolomiti golf course is reported to be one of the most beautiful and technically interesting in the Alps and is 1 km. from the site. Special rates have been agreed for guests at Baita Dolomiti. There are also other attractive golf courses within easy reach.

You might like to know
Dont miss the opportunity to visit the nearby Rio Sass canyon. Special walkways lead through the canyon, deep underground.

☑ **Cycling** (road)
☑ **Cycling** (mountain biking)
☑ **Outdoor pool**
☑ **Golf**
☑ **Rafting**
☑ **Canyoning**
☑ **Potholing**
☑ **Rock climbing**
☑ **Hiking**

Facilities: Two toilet blocks are well equipped and maintained, with a mixture of British and Turkish style WCs, controllable showers, baby room and hot water to all basins and sinks. Facilities for disabled visitors (not conveniently located). Motorcaravan service point. Bar/restaurant (all season). Swimming and paddling pools (July/Aug). Play area. Dogs are not accepted 1/8-15/9. Off site: Tourist train from site to various local villages. Golf and bicycle hire 1 km. Fishing 3 km. Riding 4 km. Canoeing. Canyoning. Walking and cycling.

Open: 1 June - 30 September.

Directions: From A22 (Brenner-Modena) take exit for S Michele/Mezzocorona. Turn right on SS43 (Val di Non) and follow signs for Cles, turning northeast after 20 km. on SS43D towards Fondo. Continue 14 km. to Sarnonico where site is signed. We are told the route from Merano via the Gampen Pass is possible. Avoid the route from Bolzano via the Mendel Pass, especially if towing. GPS: 46.41889, 11.14056

Charges guide

Per person	€ 6,80 - € 8,95
child (3-13 yrs)	€ 3,50 - € 6,80
pitch incl. electricity	€ 8,50 - € 14,80

ITALY – Rasen

Camping Residence Corones

Niederrasen 124, I-39030 Rasen (Trentino - Alto Adige)
t: 047 449 6490   e: info@corones.com
alanrogers.com/IT61990   www.corones.com

Accommodation: ☑Pitch ☑ Mobile home/chalet ☐ Hotel/B&B ☑ Apartment

Situated in a pine forest clearing at the foot of the attractive Antholz valley in the heart of German-speaking Südtirol, Corones is ideally situated both for winter sports enthusiasts and for walkers, cyclists, mountain bikers and those who prefer to explore the valleys and mountain roads of the Dolomites by car. There are 135 level pitches, all with 16A electricity and many also with water, drainage and satellite TV. The Residence offers luxury apartments and there are authentic Canadian log cabins for hire. The bar/restaurant and small shop are open all season. From the site you can see slopes which in winter become highly rated skiing pistes. A short drive up the broad Antholz/Anterselva valley takes you to an internationally important biathlon centre. An excellent day trip would be to drive up the valley and over the pass into Austria and then back via another pass. Back on site, a small pool and paddling pool could be very welcome. There is a regular programme of free excursions and occasional evening events are organised. Children's entertainment is provided in July and August.

You might like to know
There are plenty of activities on site, with something for everyone – tranquil spots for those wanting to relax in the fresh air, and many opportunities for those seeking activities and adventure. There is an activity programme for children in summer.

- ☑ Riding
- ☑ Tennis
- ☑ Golf
- ☑ Rock climbing
- ☑ Hiking
- ☑ Skiing (downhill)
- ☑ Skiing (cross-country)
- ☑ Snowboarding
- ☑ Aerial walkways
- ☑ Climbing wall
- ☑ Guided walks
- ☑ Ski safari
- ☑ Snowshoeing
- ☑ Cycling
- ☑ Fishing

Facilities: The central toilet block is traditional but well maintained and clean. Additional facilities below the Residence are of the highest quality including individual shower rooms with washbasins, washbasins with all WCs, a delightful children's unit and an excellent facility for disabled visitors. Fully equipped private shower rooms for hire. Luxurious wellness centre with saunas, solarium, jacuzzis, massage, therapy pools and heat benches. Heated outdoor swimming and paddling pools. Play area. WiFi throughout (charged). No charcoal barbecues. Off site: Tennis 800 m. Bicycle hire 1 km. Riding and fishing 3 km. Golf (9 holes) 10 km.

Open: 6 December - 7 April,
8 May - 27 October.

Directions: Rasen/Rasun is 85 km. northeast of Bolzano. From Bressanone/Brixen exit on the A22 Brenner-Modena motorway, go east on SS49 for 50 km. then turn north (signed Rasen, Antholz). Turn immediately west at roundabout in Niederrasen/Rasun di Sotto to site on left in 100 m. GPS: 46.7758, 12.0367

Charges guide

Per unit incl. 2 persons, electricity on meter	€ 21,50 - € 32,50
extra person	€ 5,50 - € 8,20
child (3-15 yrs)	€ 3,00 - € 7,50

Camping Seiser Alm

Saint Konstantin 16, I-39050 Völs am Schlern (Trentino - Alto Adige)
t: 047 170 6459 e: info@camping-seiseralm.com
alanrogers.com/IT62040 www.camping-seiseralm.com

Accommodation: ☑Pitch ☑Mobile home/chalet ☐Hotel/B&B ☑Apartment

What an amazing experience awaits you at Seiser Alm! Elisabeth and Erhard Mahlknecht have created a superb site in the magnificent Südtirol region of the Dolomite mountains. Towering peaks provide a wonderful backdrop when you dine in the charming, traditional style restaurant on the upper terrace. Here you will also find the bar, shop and reception. The 150 touring pitches are of a very high standard with 16A electricity supply, 120 with gas, water, drainage and satellite connections. Guests were delighted with the site when we visited, many coming to walk or cycle, some just to enjoy the surroundings. There are countless things to see and do here. Enjoy the grand 18-hole golf course alongside the site or join the organised excursions and activities. Local buses and cable cars provide an excellent service for summer visitors and skiers alike (discounts are available). In keeping with the natural setting, the majority of the luxury facilities are set into the hillside. Elisabeth's designs incorporating Grimm fairy tales are tastefully developed in the superb children's bathrooms that are in a magic forest setting complete with blue sky, giant mushroom and elves! If you wish for quiet, quality camping in a crystal clean environment, then visit this immaculate site.

You might like to know

The Seiser Alm campsite is located in the beautiful landscape surrounding Alpe di Siusi, with a fine view of the towering Sciliar Massif, the symbol of Alto Adige.

- ☑ Riding
- ☑ Pony trekking
- ☑ Tennis
- ☑ Cycling (road)
- ☑ Outdoor pool
- ☑ Crafts
- ☑ Golf
- ☑ Rock climbing
- ☑ Hiking
- ☑ Skiing (downhill)
- ☑ Skiing (cross-country)
- ☑ Snowboarding
- ☑ Aerial walkways
- ☑ Climbing wall
- ☑ Microlighting

Facilities: One luxury underground block is in the centre of the site. 16 private units are available. Excellent facilities for disabled visitors. Fairy tale facilities for children. Infrared sensors, underfloor heating. Washing machines and large drying room. Sauna. Supermarket. Quality restaurant and bar with terrace. Entertainment programme. Miniclub. Children's adventure park and play room. Special rooms for ski equipment. Torches useful. WiFi (charged). Apartments and mobile homes for rent. Off site: Riding. 18-hole golf course (discounts) and fishing 1 km. Bicycle hire 2 km. Buses to cable cars and ski lifts.

Open: All year excl. 2 November - 20 December.

Directions: From A22-E45 take Bolzano Nord exit. Take road for Prato Isarco/Blumau, then road for Fie/Völs. Road divides suddenly – if you miss the left fork as you enter a tunnel (Altopiano dello Sciliar/Schlerngebiet) you will pay a heavy price in extra kilometres. Enjoy the climb to Völs am Schlern and site is well signed.
GPS: 46.53344, 11.53335

Charges guide

Per unit incl. 2 persons	€ 17,30 - € 43,50
extra person	€ 6,90 - € 9,50
child (2-16 yrs)	€ 3,60 - € 7,70
electricity (per kWh)	€ 0,60

ITALY – Isolabona

Camping delle Rose

Via Provinciale, Regione Prati Gonter 4, I-18035 Isolabona (Ligúria)
t: **0184 208 130** e: **info@campingdellerose.eu**
alanrogers.com/IT64015 www.campingdellerose.eu

Accommodation: ☑Pitch ☑Mobile home/chalet ☐ Hotel/B&B ☑ Apartment

Camping delle Rose can be found close to the French border, and a few miles inland
from the Italian Riviera. This is a peaceful spot, set deep in the Maritime Alps and
surrounded by unspoilt medieval towns, picturesque churches and bustling markets.
This is a friendly, family site where Lorena, Mauro and Lorenzo, will guarantee a warm
welcome. The site is located on a terraced hillside, surrounded by eucalyptus and
mimosa. Pitches are of a good size, and most have electrical connections. A number
of mobile homes and apartments are available for rent. On-site amenities include
a swimming pool and separate paddling pool, as well as a friendly restaurant/pizzeria,
specialising in Ligurian cuisine. Delle Rose is close to the medieval village of Dolceacqua
and 6 km. from Pigna, an ancient spa town that clings to the valley sides and is famous
for its sulphurous waters. The town's main streets are arranged in concentric circles,
criss-crossed with narrow alleys, well shaded lanes and steep paths.

You might like to know
INFO Point with maps, descriptions and
brochures of the surroundings. For more
information visit our British website:
www.italycampsite.co.uk

- ☑ Riding
- ☑ Pony trekking
- ☑ Tennis
- ☑ Cycling (road)
- ☑ Cycling (mountain biking)
- ☑ Sports field
- ☑ Outdoor pool
- ☑ Sailing
- ☑ Surfing
- ☑ Windsurfing

- ☑ Diving
- ☑ Golf
- ☑ Rafting
- ☑ Canyoning
- ☑ Potholing

Facilities: Bar. Restaurant/pizzeria. Swimming
pool, paddling pool. Playground. Tourist
information. Mobile homes and chalets to rent.
Off site: Shops, cafés and restaurants in
Dolceacqua and Pigna. Monaco 32 km. San
Remo 12 km. Walking and mountain biking.
Fishing.

Open: 1 April - 31 October.

Directions: From Ventimiglia, head north on
SP54 to Dolceacqua and continue to Isolabona.
The site is well signposted from here.
GPS: 43.894573, 7.646905

Charges guide

Per unit incl. 2 persons and electricity	€ 28,50 - € 30,50
extra person	€ 8,00 - € 9,00
child (under 9 years)	€ 5,00
dog	€ 2,50

SLOVENIA – Bled

Camping Bled

Kidriceva 10c Sl, SLO-4260 Bled
t: **045 752 000** e: **info@camping-bled.com**
alanrogers.com/SV4200 www.camping-bled.com

Accommodation: ☑Pitch ☑Mobile home/chalet ☐ Hotel/B&B ☐Apartment

On the western tip of Lake Bled is Camping Bled. The waterfront here has a small public beach, immediately behind which runs a gently sloping narrow wooded valley. Pitches at the front, used mainly for overnighters, are now marked, separated by trees and enlarged, bringing the total number to 280. In areas at the back, visitors are free to pitch where they like. There is some noise from trains as they trundle out of a high tunnel overlooking the campsite on the line from Bled to Bohinj. But this is a small price to pay for the pleasure of being in a pleasant site from which the lake, its famous little island, its castle and town can be explored on foot or by boat. Unlike many other Slovenian sites, the number of statics (and semi-statics) here appears to be carefully controlled with touring caravans, motorcaravans and tents predominating.

You might like to know
There are special birdwatching and nature programmes – over 100 nesting places have been set up across the site. Binoculars and brochures illustrating the different bird species are available from reception.

☑ Riding
☑ Pony trekking
☑ Tennis
☑ Cycling *(mountain biking)*
☑ Golf
☑ Rafting
☑ Canyoning
☑ Rock climbing
☑ Hiking
☑ Aerial walkways

☑ Canoeing
☑ Kayaking
☑ Hot air ballooning
☑ Fishing
☑ Paragliding

Facilities: Toilet facilities in five blocks are of a high standard (with free hot showers). Three blocks are heated. Private bathrooms for rent. Solar energy used. Washing machines and dryers. Motorcaravan services. Gas supplies. Fridge hire. Supermarket. Restaurant. Play area and children's zoo. Games hall. Trampolines. Organised activities in July/Aug including children's club, excursions and sporting activities. Mountain bike tours. Live entertainment. Fishing. Bicycle hire. Free WiFi over site. Off site: Riding 3 km. Golf 5 km. Within walking distance of waterfront and town. Restaurants nearby.

Open: 1 April - 15 October.

Directions: From the town of Bled drive along south shore of lake to its western extremity (some 2 km) to the site.
GPS: 46.36155, 14.08075

Charges guide

Per unit incl. 2 persons and electricity	€ 21,50 - € 31,80
extra person	€ 8,90 - € 12,90
child (7-13 yrs)	€ 6,23 - € 9,03
dog	€ 3,00

Camping Terme 3000

Kranjceva ulica 12, SLO-9226 Moravske Toplice
t: **025 121 200** e: **recepcija.camp2@terme3000.si**
alanrogers.com/SV4410 www.terme3000.si

Accommodation: ☑Pitch ☐ Mobile home/chalet ☐ Hotel/B&B ☐Apartment

Camping Terme 3000 is a large site with 430 pitches. There are 200 places for touring units (all with 16A electricity), the remaining pitches being taken by seasonal campers. On a grass and gravel surface (hard tent pegs may be needed), the level, numbered pitches are of 50-100 sq.m. There are hardstandings available in the newer area of the site. The site is part of an enormous thermal spa and fun pool complex (free entry to campers) under the same name. There are over 5,000 sq.m. of water activities – swimming, jet streams, waterfalls, water massages, four water slides (the longest is 170 m) and thermal baths. The complex also provides bars and restaurants and a large golf course. Once you have had enough of the 14 indoor and outdoor pools, you could go walking or cycling through the surrounding woods and fields or try the delicious wines of the Goricko region.

You might like to know
Visit the Freerider cycle centre for bicycle hire and details of guided trips.

- ☑ Riding
- ☑ Tennis
- ☑ Cycling *(road)*
- ☑ Sports field
- ☑ Outdoor pool
- ☑ Golf
- ☑ Paintball
- ☑ Hiking
- ☑ 10-pin bowling

Facilities: Modern and clean toilet facilities provide British style toilets, open washbasins and controllable, free hot showers. Laundry facilities. Football field. Tennis. Water gymnastics. Daily activity programme for children. Golf. WiFi (charged).

Open: All year.

Directions: From Maribor, go east to Murska Sobota. From there go north towards Martjanci and then east towards Moravske Toplice. Access to the site is on the right before the bridge. Then go through a park for a further 500 m.
GPS: 46.67888, 16.22165

Charges guide

Per unit incl. 2 persons and electricity	€ 36,50 - € 40,00
extra person	€ 16,00 - € 18,00
child (6-9 yrs)	€ 8,00 - € 9,00
child (10-15 yrs)	€ 11,20 - € 12,60
dog	€ 4,00

SLOVENIA – Ptuj

Camping Terme Ptuj

Pot v toplice 9, SLO-2251 Ptuj
t: 027 494 100   e: info@terme-ptuj.si
alanrogers.com/SV4440   www.terme-ptuj.si

Accommodation: ☑Pitch ☑Mobile home/chalet ☐Hotel/B&B ☐Apartment

Camping Terme Ptuj is close to the river, just outside the interesting town of Ptuj. It is a small site with 100 level pitches, all for tourers and all with 10A electricity. In two areas, the pitches to the left are on part grass and part gravel hardstanding and are mainly used for motorcaravans. The pitches on the right-hand side are on grass under mature trees, off a circular, gravel access road. The main attraction of this site is clearly the adjacent thermal spa and fun pool complex that also attracts many local visitors. It has several slides and fun pools, as well as a sauna, solarium and spa bath. The swimming pools and saunas are free for campsite guests. This site would also be a useful stopover en-route to Croatia and the beautiful historic towns of Ptuj and Maribor are well worth a visit.

You might like to know
The thermal park has no fewer than six swimming pools and the longest water slide in Slovenia!

- ☑ Riding
- ☑ Pony trekking
- ☑ Tennis
- ☑ Cycling (road)
- ☑ Cycling (mountain biking)
- ☑ Sports field
- ☑ Outdoor pool
- ☑ Crafts
- ☑ Sailing
- ☑ Windsurfing

- ☑ Golf
- ☑ Paintball
- ☑ Skiing (downhill)
- ☑ Kayaking
- ☑ Climbing wall

Facilities: Modern toilet block with British style toilets, open washbasins and controllable, hot showers (free). En-suite facilities for disabled visitors with toilet and basin. Two washing machines. Football field. Torch useful.
Off site: Bar/restaurant and snack bar and large thermal spa 100 m.

Open: All year.

Directions: From Maribor go southeast towards Ptuj or exit the new (2009) A4 motorway at exit for Ptuj. Follow Golf/Therm signs, drive past spa/therm complex, camping is a further 100 m. GPS: 46.422683, 15.85495

Charges guide

Per unit incl. 2 persons and electricity	€ 35,00 - € 39,00
extra person	€ 15,50 - € 17,50
child (6-10 yrs)	€ 7,75 - € 8,75
dog	€ 4,00

SLOVENIA – Verzej

Camping Terme Banovci

Banovci 1A, SLO-9241 Verzej
t: 025 131 400 e: terme@terme-banovci.si
alanrogers.com/SV4445 www.terme-banovci.si

Accommodation: ☑Pitch ☑Mobile home/chalet ☐Hotel/B&B ☐Apartment

Terme Banovci is a comfortable, quiet, countryside site with 130 normal touring pitches plus 50 FKK naturist pitches, which are located separately. The grassed pitches have ample shade, are accessed by gravel roads and all have 10A electricity. Entry to the indoor (35-38°C) and outdoor (25-27°C) pools with a total surface area of 2,000 square metres is free to campers. The pools with large outdoor slide and ample space for sunbathing are all that one expects from a modern, well equipped, thermal spa. The comfortable restaurant is built in traditional style, and drinks and food are available on the terrace beside the pool. The indoor pool contains thermal mineral water, which is pumped up from a depth of 1,700 m. The water is rich in fluorides and recognised as being beneficial in treating rheumatism and other ailments. The outdoor pool is filled with normal water and is equipped with underwater massage jets, whirlpools, a waterfall and water slide. In addition, there is a children's paddling pool.

You might like to know
Please note: this is partly a naturist campsite, the first in Europe to be developed around a thermal complex.

☑ Riding
☑ Tennis
☑ Cycling (road)
☑ Outdoor pool
☑ Crafts
☑ Archery
☑ Paintball
☑ Rafting
☑ Fishing

Facilities: Two well appointed, heated sanitary blocks. Washbasins in cabins. Facilities for disabled visitors. Laundry. Motorcaravan service point. Nordic walking. Volleyball. Tennis. Morning gymnastics. Entertainment programme. Wellness centre with three Finnish saunas. Solarium. Turkish bath. Various massage programmes (at extra cost). Off site: Numerous walking and cycling paths.

Open: 1 April - 6 November.

Directions: Site is 38 km. east of Maribor. From A5 take Vucja Vas exit and head south on 230 for 5 km. to Knzevci pri Ljutomeru. Then turn northeast on 439 for 1 km. and fork right to Banovci. Site is 400 m. northeast of Banovci and signed in village. GPS: 46.573181, 16.171494

Charges guide

Per unit incl. 2 persons and electricity	€ 27,50 - € 29,50
dog	€ 3,00

Camping Sobec

Sobceva cesta 25, SLO-4248 Lesce
t: 045 353 700   e: sobec@siol.net
alanrogers.com/SV4210   www.sobec.si

Accommodation: ☑Pitch ☑Mobile home/chalet ☐Hotel/B&B ☐Apartment

Sobec is situated in a valley between the Julian Alps and the Karavanke Mountains, in a pine grove between the Sava Dolinka river and a small lake. It is only 3 km. from Bled and 20 km. from the Karavanke Tunnel. There are 500 unmarked pitches on level, grassy fields off tarmac access roads (450 for touring units), all with 16A electricity. Shade is provided by mature pine trees and younger trees separate some pitches. Camping Sobec is surrounded by water – the Sava river borders it on three sides and on the fourth is a small, artificial lake with grassy fields for sunbathing. Some pitches have views over the lake, which has an enclosed area providing safe swimming for children. This site is a good base for an active holiday, since both the Sava Dolinka and the Sava Bohinjka rivers are suitable for canoeing, kayaking, rafting and fishing, whilst the nearby mountains offer challenges for mountain climbing, paragliding and canyoning.

You might like to know

Just 4 km. from the campsite, a tourist airport provides an aerotaxi service enabling you to visit the surrounding area by air.

☑ Riding
☑ Cycling *(mountain biking)*
☑ Golf
☑ Rafting
☑ Canyoning
☑ Hiking
☑ Kayaking
☑ Fishing
☑ Beach volleyball
☑ Minigolf

Facilities: Three traditional style toilet blocks (all now refurbished) with mainly British style toilets, washbasins in cabins and controllable hot showers. Child size toilets and basins. Well equipped baby room. Facilities for disabled visitors. Laundry facilities. Motorcaravan service point. Supermarket, bar/restaurant with stage for live performances. Playgrounds. Rafting, canyoning and kayaking organised. Miniclub. Tours to Bled and the Triglav National Park organised. WiFi throughout (free).
Off site: Golf and riding 2 km.

Open: 14 April - 30 September.

Directions: Site is off the main road from Lesce to Bled and is well signed just outside Lesce. GPS: 46.35607, 14.14992

Charges guide

Per unit incl. 2 persons and electricity	€ 24,70 - € 30,10
extra person	€ 10,60 - € 13,30
child (7-14 yrs)	€ 7,90 - € 9,90
dog	€ 3,50

SLOVENIA – Kobarid

Kamp Koren Kobarid

Ladra 1b, SLO-5222 Kobarid
t: 053 891 311   e: info@kamp-koren.si
alanrogers.com/SV4270   www.kamp-koren.si

Accommodation: ☑Pitch ☑Mobile home/chalet ☐ Hotel/B&B ☐Apartment

Superbly run by its owner, Lidija Koren, this peaceful, well shaded site is located above the Soca river gorge in the countryside close to Kobarid. A small site with 90 pitches, it is deservedly very popular with those interested in outdoor sports, including hiking, mountain biking, paragliding, canoeing, canyoning, rafting and fishing. At the same time, its quiet location makes it a good site for those seeking a relaxing break. Six attractive, well equipped chalets are a recent addition (2009). The Julian Alps, and in particular the Triglav National Park, is a wonderful and under-explored part of Slovenia that has much to offer. Kobarid, probably best approached via Udine in Italy, is a pleasant country town, with easy access to nearby rivers, valleys and mountains, which alone justify a visit to Kamp Koren. But most British visitors will remember it for the opportunity it provides to fill that curious gap in their knowledge of European history. The local museum in Kobarid was recently voted European Museum of the Year and is excellent.

You might like to know

Near Kamp Koren you can enjoy skiing on Kanin. Kanin-Sella Nevea is the only high-mountain ski resort in Slovenia where the pistes rise over 2,000 metres. The resort lies above Bovec, on the banks of the Soca river.

- ☑ **Cycling** (road)
- ☑ **Cycling** (mountain biking)
- ☑ **Rafting**
- ☑ **Canyoning**
- ☑ **Rock climbing**
- ☑ **Hiking**
- ☑ **Skiing** (downhill)
- ☑ **Skiing** (cross-country)
- ☑ **Canoeing**
- ☑ **Fishing**

Facilities: Two attractive and well maintained log-built toilet blocks. Facilities for disabled visitors. Laundry facilities. Motorcaravan services. Shop (March-Nov). Café dispenses light meals, snacks and drinks apparently with flexible closing hours. Sauna. Play area. Bowling. Fishing. Bicycle hire. Canoe hire. Climbing walls for adults. Communal barbecue. WiFi. Off site: Town within walking distance. Riding 5 km. Golf 20 km. Guided tours in the Soca valley and around Slovenia start from the campsite.

Open: All year.

Directions: Approaching Kobarid from Tolmin on 102, just before Kobarid turn right on 203 towards Bovec and after 100 m. take descending slip road to right and keep more or less straight on to Napoléon's bridge (about 500 m). Cross bridge and site is on left, 100 m. GPS: 46.25075, 13.58658

Charges guide

Per unit incl. 2 persons and electricity	€ 23,00 - € 26,00
dog	€ 2,00

Balatontourist Camping Füred

Széchenyi út 24., H-8230 Balatonfüred (Veszprem County)
t: 87 580 241 e: fured@balatontourist.hu
alanrogers.com/HU5090 www.balatontourist.hu

Accommodation: ☑Pitch ☑Mobile home/chalet ☑Hotel/B&B ☑Apartment

This is a large international holiday village rather than just a campsite. It offers a very wide range of facilities and sporting activities. All that one could want for a family holiday can be found here. The 890 individual pitches (60-120 sq.m), all with electricity (6/10A), are on either side of hard access roads on which pitch numbers are painted. Many bungalows are for rent. Mature trees cover about two thirds of the site giving shade, with the remaining area being in the open. Directly on the lake with 800 m. of access for boats and bathing, there is a large, grassy area for relaxation, a small beach area for children and a variety of watersports. A water ski drag lift is most spectacular with its four towers erected in the lake to pull skiers around the circuit. There is a swimming pool on site with lifeguards. Along the main road that runs through the site are shops and kiosks, with the main bar/restaurant and terrace overlooking the lake. Other bars and restaurants are around the site. The site is part of the Balatontourist organisation and, while public access is allowed for the amenities, security is good. Some tour operators – Danish and German.

You might like to know

Lake Balaton is the largest lake in Central Europe and popular with anglers. Swimming is allowed, and at the height of summer the water temperature can reach 24-26°C.

☑ Riding
☑ Tennis
☑ Cycling (road)
☑ Outdoor pool
☑ Sailing
☑ Windsurfing
☑ Diving
☑ Waterskiing
☑ Fishing
☑ Free water slide

Facilities: Five fully equipped toilet blocks around the site include hot water for dishwashing and laundry (cleaning and maintenance variable). Private cabins for rent. Laundry service. Numerous bars, restaurants, cafés, food bars and supermarket (15/5-15/9). Stalls and kiosks with wide range of goods and souvenirs. Excellent swimming pool (1/6-31/8). Sandy beach. Large free water chute. Animation for children. Sports activities organised for adults. Sauna. Fishing. Water ski lift. Windsurf school. Sailing. Pedalos. Play area. Tennis. Minigolf. Video games. Bicycle hire. WiFi throughout (charged). Dogs are not accepted. Off site: A street of fast food bars with outdoor terraces under trees. Riding and golf 10 km.

Open: 27 April - 30 September.

Directions: Site is just south of Balatonfüred, at the traffic circle on Balatonfüred-Tihany road is well signed. Gates closed 13.00-15.00 except at weekends. GPS: 46.94565, 17.87709

Charges guide

Per unit incl. 2 persons and electricity	HUF 3600 - 9200
extra person	HUF 800 - 1600
child (2-14 yrs)	HUF 500 - 1200

Martfü Health & Recreation Centre

Tüzép út, H-5435 Martfü (Jász-Nagkyun-Szolnok County)
t: **56 580 531** e: **martfu@camping.hu**
alanrogers.com/HU5255 www.martfu-turizmus.hu

Accommodation: ☑Pitch ☑Mobile home/chalet ☐ Hotel/B&B ☐Apartment

The Martfü campsite is a modern site with 61 touring pitches on grassy terrain with rubber hardstandings. Each is around 90 sq.m. and separated by young bushes and trees. All have electricity (16/25A), waste water drainage, cable and satellite TV. There is a water tap per two pitches. There is no shade as yet, which may cause the site to become a real suntrap in summer, when temperatures may rise up to 34 degrees. A small lake and its beach on the site will cool you off. The main attraction at this site is the thermal spa, which is said to aid people with skin and rheumatic problems. Martfü is right on the banks of the River Tisza, which also makes it an excellent spot for those who enjoy watersports and fishing. The village of Martfü is close with numerous shops, restaurants and bars.

You might like to know
There is an excellent local spa and wellness centre.

- ☑ Riding
- ☑ Pony trekking
- ☑ Tennis
- ☑ Cycling (road)
- ☑ Cycling (mountain biking)
- ☑ Sailing
- ☑ Golf
- ☑ Hiking
- ☑ Canoeing
- ☑ Fishing

Facilities: Two modern, heated toilet blocks with British style toilets, open style washbasins, and free, controllable hot showers. Children's toilet and shower. Heated baby room. En-suite facilities for disabled visitors. Laundry. Kitchen with cooking rings. Motorcaravan services. Shop for basics. Takeaway for bread and drinks. Welcoming bar with satellite TV and WiFi. Indoor and outdoor swimming pools. Bowling. Library. Sauna. Jacuzzi. Playing field. Tennis. Minigolf. Fishing. Bicycle hire. Watersports. English is spoken. Off site: Fishing 50 m. Boat launching 1.5 km. Riding 5 km.

Open: All year.

Directions: Driving into Martfü from the north on the 442 road, take the first exit at the roundabout (site is signed). Continue for 800 m. and site is signed on the right.
GPS: 47.019933, 20.268517

Charges guide

Per person	HUF 1200
child (6-14 yrs)	HUF 600
pitch	HUF 900 - 1200

No credit cards.

HUNGARY – Révfülöp

Balatontourist Camping Napfény

Halász ut. 5, H-8253 Révfülöp (Veszprem County)
t: **87 563 031** e: **napfeny@balatontourist.hu**
alanrogers.com/HU5370 www.balatontourist.hu

Accommodation: ☑Pitch ☑Mobile home/chalet ☐Hotel/B&B ☐Apartment

Camping Napfény, an exceptionally good site, is designed for families with children of all ages looking for an active holiday, and has a 200 m. frontage on Lake Balaton. The site's 370 pitches vary in size (60-110 sq.m) and almost all have shade – very welcome during the hot Hungarian summers – and 6-10A electricity. As with most of the sites on Lake Balaton, a train line runs just outside the site boundary. There are steps to get into the lake and canoes, boats and pedaloes for hire. An extensive entertainment programme is designed for all ages and there are several bars and restaurants of various styles. There are souvenir shops and a supermarket. In fact, you need not leave the site at all during your holiday, although there are several excursions on offer, including to Budapest or to one of the many Hungarian spas, a trip over Lake Balaton or a traditional wine tour.

You might like to know
Camping Napfény is very child friendly with plenty of activities aimed at younger guests, including a new paddling pool.

☑ Cycling *(road)*
☑ Sports field
☑ Windsurfing
☑ Kayaking
☑ Pedaloes
☑ Fishing
☑ Free water slide
☑ Trampoline
☑ Beach volleyball
☑ Table tennis

Facilities: The three excellent sanitary blocks have toilets, washbasins (open style and in cabins) with hot and cold water, spacious showers (both preset and controllable), child size toilets and basins, and two bathrooms (hourly charge). Heated baby room. Facilities for disabled campers. Launderette. Dog shower. Motorcaravan services. Supermarket, souvenir shop and several bars (all 1/6-31/8). Restaurants. Children's pool. Sports field. Minigolf. Fishing. Bicycle hire. Canoe, rowing boats and pedalo hire. Extensive entertainment programme for all ages. WiFi throughout (charged). Off site: Tennis 300 m. Riding 3 km. Golf 20 km.

Open: 27 April - 30 September.

Directions: Follow road 71 from Veszprém southeast to Keszthely. Site is in Révfülöp. GPS: 46.829469, 17.640164

Charges guide

Per unit incl. 2 persons and electricity	HUF 3600 - 7150
extra person	HUF 850 - 1200
child (2-14 yrs)	HUF 550 - 950
dog	HUF 550 - 950

AUSTRIA – Raggal

Camping Grosswalsertal

Plazera 21, A-6741 Raggal (Vorarlberg)
t: 055 532 09 e: info@camping-austria.info
alanrogers.com/AU0015 www.camping-austria.info

Accommodation: ☑ Pitch ☐ Mobile home/chalet ☐ Hotel/B&B ☑ Apartment

As we climbed up to this site we seemed to be above the clouds. We then descended into a beautiful green valley and saw the site on a flat plateau below. From almost every pitch there are the most fantastic views down the valley. On open grass, there are 55 slightly sloping, un-numbered and unmarked pitches all with 16A electricity. Plenty of sporting activities are available locally and there are many places to visit, as well as walks and bike rides in the immediate area. Alternatively, just rest on the site and watch the clouds roll by. The site is very popular with Dutch visitors. When we arrived, Siegmar Zech, the owner was busy siting a caravan, so we followed the sound of happy children and campers playing. Our immediate impressions were that this is a good site and one from which you could base an excellent holiday.

You might like to know

This campsite is located on a high plateau at the centre of the Grosses Walsertal biosphere park (875 m. above sea level). There are stunning and rarely equalled views of the surrounding villages and the Walserberge mountains.

☑ **Riding**
☑ **Cycling** (road)
☑ **Cycling** (mountain biking)
☑ **Outdoor pool**
☑ **Rafting**
☑ **Rock climbing**
☑ **Hiking**
☑ **Skiing** (downhill)
☑ **Skiing** (cross-country)
☑ **Fishing**

Facilities: The modern sanitary block has ample and clean toilets, hot showers and washbasins. Washing machine and dryer. Small shop with essential supplies. Swimming pool (1/6-15/9). Play area. Bicycle hire. WiFi. Off site: Fishing and riding 2 km. Golf 14 km.

Open: 1 May - 30 September.

Directions: From the A14 take exit 50 for Nenzing and Gr. Walsertal and proceed to Bludesch. Turn left toward Raggal where you take the left fork, pass a Spar supermarket and 2 km. downhill to the site.
GPS: 47.21585, 9.8537

Charges guide

Per unit incl. 2 persons and electricity	€ 18,50 - € 21,50
extra person	€ 5,00
child (0-13 yrs)	€ 2,00 - € 3,50
dog	€ 2,00

No credit cards.

AUSTRIA – Ehrwald

Ferienanlage Tiroler Zugspitze

Obermoos 1, A-6632 Ehrwald (Tirol)
t: **056 732 309** e: **welcome@zugspitze-resort.at**
alanrogers.com/AU0040 www.zugspitze-resort.at

Accommodation: ☑Pitch ☐ Mobile home/chalet ☑Hotel/B&B ☑Apartment

Although Ehrwald is in Austria, it is from the entrance of Tiroler Zugspitze that a cable car runs to the summit of Germany's highest mountain. Standing at 1,200 feet above sea level at the foot of the mountain, the 200 pitches (120 for touring), mainly of stones over grass, are on flat terraces with fine panoramic views in parts. All have 16A electricity connections. The modern reception building at the entrance also houses a fine restaurant with a terrace which is open to those using the cable car, as well as those staying on the site. There are some 30 pitches outside the barrier for late arrivals and overnighters. A further large modern building, heated in cool weather, has indoor and outdoor pools, sauna, minigym and wellness centre. This excellent mountain site, with its superb facilities, provides a good base from which to explore this interesting part of Austria and Bavaria by car or on foot. A trip up to the Zugspitze offers beautiful views and many opportunities for mountain walking.

You might like to know

The Tiroler Zugspitzbahn cable car will take you to the summit of the Zugspitze, from where you can enjoy the breathtaking views while dining at the summit restaurant.

- ☑ Cycling *(road)*
- ☑ Cycling *(mountain biking)*
- ☑ Outdoor pool
- ☑ Golf
- ☑ Rafting
- ☑ Rock climbing
- ☑ Hiking
- ☑ Fitness/gym
- ☑ Fishing

Facilities: A good sanitary block provides some washbasins in cabins and 20 private bathrooms for rent. Separate baby and toddler unit. Facilities for disabled visitors. Laundry facilities. Drying rooms. Motorcaravan service point. Dog washing area. Shop. Bar. Restaurant. Indoor pool with sauna, whirlpool. Fitness centre with solarium and massage room. Outdoor pool and children's pool with slide. Internet access. Bicycle loan and motor scooters for hire. Play area. Organised activities in season. Off site: Hotel, souvenir shop and cable car 100 m. Sports in Ehrwald 5 km.

Open: 1 January - Easter, 28 May - 31 October, mid - end December.

Directions: Carefully follow signs in Ehrwald to Tiroler Zugspitzbahn and then signs to site. GPS: 47.42521, 10.93809

Charges guide

Per person	€ 10,00 - € 12,00
child (4-15 yrs)	€ 7,50 - € 8,50
pitch	€ 6,00 - € 8,00
electricity per kWh.	€ 0,80
dog	€ 4,00

AUSTRIA – Längenfeld

Camping Ötztal Längenfeld

Unterlangenfeld 220, A-6444 Längenfeld (Tirol)
t: 052 535 348 e: info@camping-oetztal.com
alanrogers.com/AU0045 www.camping-oetztal.com

Accommodation: ☑Pitch ☑Mobile home/chalet ☐ Hotel/B&B ☐Apartment

Camping Ötztal Längenfeld, a family run site, is situated some 400 metres from the pretty village of Längenfeld, at the edge of a forest. Next door are the local sports centre and swimming pool, and a restaurant. In summer, the campsite is ideal for walking and cycling, as well as mountaineering tours. In the winter you can enjoy cross-country skiing right from the doorstep and a free bus shuttle operates to the Ötztal Ski arena. The site provides 200 level grass pitches of which 150 are for tourers. All pitches have electricity and 100 also have gas, water, drainage and a TV point.

You might like to know

Längenfeld is located at an altitude of 1,173 m. at the centre of the Ötztal valley and extends across a 20 km.-long plain. There are 110 km. of signposted running trails. This altitude is perfect for gentle high-altitude training and there is an excellent range of trails to choose from.

- ☑ Cycling *(road)*
- ☑ Cycling *(mountain biking)*
- ☑ Rafting
- ☑ Canyoning
- ☑ Rock climbing
- ☑ Hiking
- ☑ Skiing *(downhill)*
- ☑ Skiing *(cross-country)*
- ☑ Canoeing
- ☑ Fishing

Facilities: Excellent sanitary facilities include four bathrooms to rent for private use. Baby room. Facilities for disabled visitors. Female hairdressing room. Dog shower. Washing machines and dryer. Ski room. Motorcaravan service point. Restaurant serves breakfast and takeaway. Sauna and solarium. WiFi. Off site: Sports centre and swimming pool adjacent (reduced prices for campers). Längenfeld and Aqua Dome thermal spa facility. Bicycle hire 0.5 km.

Open: All year.

Directions: From A12 take exit 123 and follow the 186 along the Ötztal Valley towards Sölden for 20 km. On entering Längenfeld, continue up hill into town and shortly after tourist information office on right there are signs for site. Enter through yard and follow lane past sports centre to entrance. GPS: 47.07229, 10.96431

Charges guide

Per unit incl. 2 persons and electricity (plus meter)	€ 19,90 - € 29,00
extra person	€ 6,20 - € 7,30
child (4-13 yrs)	€ 4,50 - € 5,50
dog	€ 2,60

No credit cards.

AUSTRIA – Natters

Ferienparadies Natterer See

Natterer See 1, A-6161 Natters (Tirol)
t: 051 254 6732 e: info@natterersee.com
alanrogers.com/AU0060 www.natterersee.com

Accommodation: ☑Pitch ☑Mobile home/chalet ☐Hotel/B&B ☐Apartment

In a quiet location arranged around two lakes and set amidst beautiful alpine scenery, this site founded in 1930 is renowned as one of Austria's top sites. Over the last few years many improvements have been carried out and pride of place goes to the innovative, award-winning, multifunctional building at the entrance to the site. This contains all of the sanitary facilities expected of a top site, including a special section for children, private bathrooms to rent and also a dog bath. The reception, shop, café/bar/bistro and cinema are on the ground floor, and on the upper floor is a panoramic lounge where the owner has assembled the largest collection of model camping cars and caravans in Europe. Almost all of the 235 pitches are for tourers. They are terraced, set on gravel/grass, all have electricity and most offer a splendid view of the mountains. The site's lakeside restaurant with bar and large terrace has a good menu and is the ideal place to spend the evening. With a bus every hour and the city centre only 19 minutes away this is also a good site from which to visit Innsbruck.

You might like to know
The campsite is open all year around and is situated close to the city of Innsbruck, a former Winter Olympic Games city.

- ☑ Riding
- ☑ Tennis
- ☑ Cycling (mountain biking)
- ☑ Golf
- ☑ Skiing (downhill)
- ☑ Curling
- ☑ Ice skating
- ☑ Ice hockey
- ☑ Sail boats
- ☑ Paragliding

Facilities: The large sanitary block has underfloor heating, some private cabins, plus excellent facilities for babies, children and disabled visitors. Laundry facilities. Motorcaravan services. Fridge box hire. Bar. Restaurant and takeaway with at least one open all year. Pizzeria. Good shop. Playgrounds. Children's activity programme. Day nursery in high season. Sports field. Archery. Youth room with games, pool and billiards. TV room with Sky. Open-air cinema. Mountain bike hire. Aquapark (1/5-30/9). Surf bikes and pedaloes. Canoes and mini sailboats for rent. Fishing. Entertainment programme (mid May-mid Oct). Dogs are not accepted in high season (July/Aug). WiFi (charged). Off site: Tennis and minigolf nearby. Riding 6 km. Golf 12 km.

Open: All year.

Directions: From Inntal autobahn (A12) take Brenner autobahn (A13) to Innsbruck-sud/Natters exit (no. 3). Turn left by Shell petrol station onto B182 to Natters. At roundabout take first exit and immediately right again and follow signs to site 4 km. Do not use sat nav for final approach to site, follow signs. GPS: 47.23755, 11.34201

Charges guide

Per unit incl. 2 persons and electricity	€ 23,40 - € 34,60
extra person	€ 5,90 - € 8,30

Aktiv-Camping Prutz Tirol

Pontlatzstrasse 22, A-6522 Prutz (Tirol)
t: 054 722 648 e: info@aktiv-camping.at
alanrogers.com/AU0155 www.aktiv-camping.at

Accommodation: ☑Pitch ☑Mobile home/chalet ☐Hotel/B&B ☐Apartment

Aktiv-Camping is a long site which lies beside, and is fenced off from, the River Inn. Most of the 100 individual level pitches are for touring and are 80 sq.m. They all have 6A electrical connections and in the larger area fit together sideways and back to back. As a result, the site can sometimes have the appearance of being quite crowded. There is a separate overnight area for motorcaravans. This is an attractive area with many activities in both summer and winter for all age groups. You may well consider using this site not just as an overnight stop, but also for a longer stay. From Roman times onwards, when the Via Augusta passed through, this border region's strategic importance has left behind many fortifications that today feature among its many tourist attractions. Others include rambling, cycling and mountain biking, swimming in lakes and pools as well interesting, educational and adventurous activities for children. The Tiroler Summer card, available without charge at reception, has free offers and discounts for many attractions; in addition the booklet Wonderful Holiday Bliss, free at reception, contains a wealth of useful tourist information.

You might like to know
Hikers will be rewarded with a wonderful view from the Kaunertaler glacier.

☑ **Riding**
☑ **Tennis**
☑ **Cycling** (mountain biking)
☑ **Outdoor pool**
☑ **Rock climbing**
☑ **Skiing** (downhill)
☑ **Snowboarding**
☑ **Pedaloes**
☑ **Fishing**
☑ **Nordic walking**

Facilities: The sanitary facilities are of a high standard, with private cabins and good facilities for disabled visitors. Baby room. Washing machine. Dog shower. Small shop (all year). Bar (15/5-15/9). Takeaway (15/5-15/9). Play room. Ski room. Skating rink. Children's entertainment. Guided walks, skiing (free shuttle service). WiFi throughout. Off site: Riding 1 km. Indoor pool at Feichten, Pilgrim's Church at Kaltenbrunn. Kaunertaler Glacier.

Open: All year.

Directions: Travelling west from Innsbruck on the E60/A12 for 65 km. Exit at Landeck and follow the B315 (direction Reschenpass) turn south onto the B180 signed Bregenz, Arlberg, Innsbruck and Fern Pass for 11 km. to Prutz. Site is signed to the right from the B180 over the bridge. GPS: 47.08833, 10.65831

Charges guide

Per unit incl. 2 persons and electricity	€ 16,00 - € 25,90
extra person	€ 4,00 - € 7,20
child (5-14 yrs)	€ 2,50 - € 4,00
dog	€ 2,50 - € 3,50

AUSTRIA – Bruck

Sportcamp Woferlgut

Kroessenbach 40, A-5671 Bruck (Salzburg)
t: 065 457 3030 e: info@sportcamp.at
alanrogers.com/AU0180 www.sportcamp.at

Accommodation: ☑Pitch ☑Mobile home/chalet ☐ Hotel/B&B ☐Apartment

The village of Bruck lies at the junction of the B311 and the Grossglocknerstrasse in the Hohe Tauern National Park. Sportcamp Woferlgut, a family run site, is one of the best in Austria. Surrounded by mountains, the site is quite flat with pleasant views. The 350 level, grass pitches are marked out by shrubs (300 for touring units) and each has 16A electricity (Europlug), water, drainage, cable TV socket and gas point. A high grass bank separates the site and the road. The site's own lake, used for swimming and fishing, is surrounded by a landscaped sunbathing area. A free activity and entertainment programme is provided all year round. This includes live music evenings, a club for children, weekly barbecues and guided cycle and mountain tours. The fitness centre has a fully equipped gym, whilst another building contains a sauna and cold dip, Turkish bath, solarium (all free) massage (charged) and a bar. In winter, a cross-country skiing trail and toboggan run lead from the site and a free bus service is provided to nearby skiing facilities. With Salzburg to the north and Innsbruck to the northwest, this is a splendid base for a family holiday. Good English is spoken.

You might like to know
Open all year. In winter there are more than 90 ski lifts within 10 km. of the campsite.

☑ Tennis
☑ Cycling (mountain biking)
☑ Outdoor pool
☑ Sailing
☑ Golf
☑ Hiking
☑ Skiing (downhill)
☑ Skiing (cross-country)
☑ Fitness/gym
☑ Fishing

Facilities: Three modern sanitary blocks (the newest in a class of its own) have excellent facilities, including private cabins, underfloor heating and music. Washing machines and dryers. Facilities for disabled visitors. Family bathrooms for hire. Motorcaravan services. Well stocked shop. Bar, restaurant and takeaway. Small, heated outdoor pool and children's pool (1/5-15/10). Fitness centre. Two playgrounds, indoor play room and children's cinema. Tennis. Bicycle hire. Fishing. Watersports and lake swimming. Collection of small animals with pony rides for young children. Adventure golf course. WiFi throughout (charged). Off site: Riding 1.5 km. Skiing 2.5 km. Golf 3 km. Boat launching and sailing 3.5 km. Hiking and skiing (all year).

Open: All year.

Directions: Site is southwest of Bruck. From road B311, Bruck bypass, take southern exit (Grossglockner) and site is signed from the junction of B311 and B107 roads (small signs). GPS: 47.2838, 12.81694

Charges guide

Per unit incl. 2 persons and electricity (plus meter)	€ 23,00 - € 32,80
extra person	€ 5,40 - € 8,70
child (2-10 yrs)	€ 4,30 - € 6,40

Camping Grassi

Grassiweg 60, CH-3714 Frutigen (Bern)
t: 033 671 1149 e: campinggrassi@bluewin.ch
alanrogers.com/CH9360 www.camping-grassi.ch

Accommodation: ☑Pitch ☑Mobile home/chalet ☐ Hotel/B&B ☐Apartment

This is a small site with about half the pitches occupied by static caravans, used by their owners for weekends and holidays. The 70 or so places available for touring units are not marked out but it is said that the site is not allowed to become overcrowded. Most places are on level grass with two small terraces at the end of the site. There is little shade but the site is set in a river valley with trees on the hills which enclose the area. Electricity is available for all pitches but long leads may be required in parts. It would make a useful overnight stop en-route for Kandersteg and the railway station where cars can join the train for transportation through the Lotschberg Tunnel to the Rhône Valley and Simplon Pass, or for a longer stay to explore the Bernese Oberland.

You might like to know
Some typically Tirolean sports can be enjoyed at a nearby adventure park.

☑ Tennis
☑ Cycling (road)
☑ Cycling (mountain biking)
☑ Outdoor pool
☑ Crafts
☑ Rock climbing
☑ Hiking
☑ Skiing (downhill)
☑ Snowboarding
☑ Fishing

Facilities: The well constructed, heated sanitary block is of good quality. Washing machine and dryer. Gas supplies. Motorcaravan services. Communal room with TV. Kiosk (1/7-31/8). Play area and play house. Mountain bike hire. Fishing. Bicycle hire. WiFi. Off site: Shops and restaurants 10 minutes walk away in village. Riding 2 km. Outdoor and indoor pools, tennis and minigolf in Frutigen. A new sauna and wellness centre has recently opened in the village. Skiing and walking.

Open: All year.

Directions: Take Kandersteg road from Spiez and leave at Frutigen Dorf exit from where site is signed. GPS: 46.58173, 7.64219

Charges guide

Per unit incl. 2 persons and electricity	CHF 25,80 - 32,30
extra person	CHF 6,40
child (1-16 yrs)	CHF 1,50 - 3,20
dog	CHF 1,50

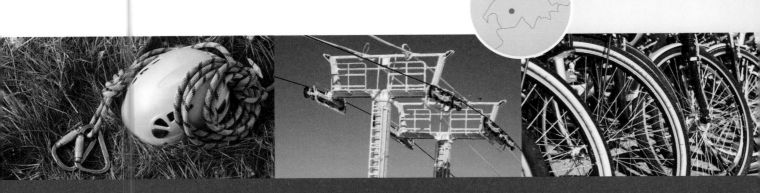

SWITZERLAND – Interlaken-Thunersee

Camping Manor Farm 1

Seestrassee 201, CH-3800 Interlaken-Thunersee (Bern)
t: 033 822 2264   e: manorfarm1@swisscamps.ch
alanrogers.com/CH9420   www.manorfarm.ch

Accommodation: ☑Pitch ☑Mobile home/chalet ☐Hotel/B&B ☐Apartment

Manor Farm has been popular with British visitors for many years, as this is one of the traditional touring areas of Switzerland. The flat terrain is divided into 525 individual, numbered pitches which vary considerably, both in size (60-100 sq.m) and price. There is shade in some places. There are 144 pitches with electricity (4/13A), water and drainage, and 55 also have cable TV connections. Reservations can be made, although you should find space, except perhaps in late July/early August when the best places may be taken. Around 40 per cent of the pitches are taken by permanent or letting units and a tour operator. The site lies outside the town on the northern side of the Thuner See, with most of the site between the road and lake but with one part on the far side of the road. Interlaken is very much a tourist town, but the area is rich in scenery with innumerable mountain excursions and walks available. The lakes and Jungfrau railway are near at hand. Manor Farm is a large campsite, efficiently run with a minimum of formality and would suit those looking for an active family holiday.

You might like to know
The campsite is located on the shores of Lake Thun amid beautiful mountain scenery and with numerous opportunities for watersports and excursions. Also open in winter.

- ☑ Riding
- ☑ Cycling (road)
- ☑ Outdoor pool
- ☑ Sailing
- ☑ Windsurfing
- ☑ Golf
- ☑ Hiking
- ☑ Fishing

Facilities: Seven separate toilet blocks are practical, heated and fully equipped. Twenty private toilet units are for rent. Laundry facilities. Motorcaravan services. Gas supplies. Excellent shop (1/4-15/10). Site-owned restaurant adjacent (1/3-30/10). Snack bar with takeaway (1/7-20/8). TV room. Playground and paddling pool. Minigolf. Bicycle hire. Sailing and windsurfing school. Lake swimming. Boat hire (slipway for campers' own). Fishing. Daily activity and entertainment programme in high season. Excursions. Max. 1 dog. WiFi (charged). Off site: Golf (18 holes) 500 m. (handicap card). Riding 3 km. Good area for cycling and walking.

Open: All year.

Directions: Site is 3 km. west of Interlaken along the road running north of the Thuner See towards Thun. Follow signs for 'Camp 1'. From A8 (bypassing Interlaken) take exit 24 marked Gunten, Beatenberg, which is a spur road bringing you out close to site.
GPS: 46.68129, 7.81524

Charges guide

Per unit incl. 2 persons and electricity	CHF 37,00 - 63,50
extra person	CHF 10,50
child (6-15 yrs)	CHF 5,00

Camping Lazy Rancho 4

Lehnweg 6, CH-3800 Unterseen-Interlaken (Bern)
t: 033 822 8716 e: info@lazyrancho.ch
alanrogers.com/CH9430 www.lazyrancho.ch

Accommodation: ☑Pitch ☑Mobile home/chalet ☐ Hotel/B&B ☐Apartment

This super site is in a quiet location with fantastic views of the dramatic mountains of Eiger, Monch and Jungfrau. Neat, orderly and well maintained, the site is situated in a wide valley just 1 km. from Lake Thun and 1.5 km. from Interlaken. The English speaking owners lovingly care for the site and will endeavour to make you feel very welcome. Connected by gravel roads, the 155 pitches, of which 90 are for touring units, are on well tended level grass (some with hardstanding, all with 10A electricity). There are 28 pitches also with water and waste water drainage. This is a quiet, friendly site, popular with British visitors. The owners offer advice on day trips out, and how to get the best bargains on the railway.

You might like to know
The summit of the Niesen Mountain can be reached by funicular railway; from there you can enjoy the great views of Lake Thun and the Bernese Oberland.

- ☑ Riding
- ☑ Cycling (road)
- ☑ Cycling (mountain biking)
- ☑ Golf
- ☑ Rafting
- ☑ Canyoning
- ☑ Rock climbing
- ☑ Fishing
- ☑ Parachuting
- ☑ Paragliding

Facilities: Two good sanitary blocks are both heated with free hot showers, good facilities for disabled campers and a baby room. Laundry. Campers' kitchen with microwave, cooker, fridge and utensils. Motorcaravan service point. Well stocked shop. TV and games room. Play area. Small swimming pool. Bicycle hire (June-Aug). Free WiFi. Free bus in the Interlaken area – bus stop is five minutes walk from site. Off site: Cycle trails and waymarked footpaths. Riding 500 m. Golf and bicycle hire 1 km. Fishing 1 km. Boat launching 1.5 km. Interlaken and leisure centre 2 km.

Open: 1 May - 20 October.

Directions: Site is on north side of Lake Thun. From road 8 (Thun-Interlaken) on south side of lake take exit 24 Interlaken West. Follow towards lake at roundabout then follow signs for campings. Lazy Rancho is Camp 4. The last 500 m. is a little narrow but no problem. GPS: 46.68605, 7.830633

Charges guide

Per unit incl. 2 persons and electricity	CHF 30,50 - 54,50
extra person	CHF 6,00 - 8,00
child (6-15 yrs)	CHF 3,50 - 4,80
dog	free - CHF 3,00

Camping Jungfrau

CH-3822 Lauterbrunnen (Bern)
t: 033 856 2010   e: info@camping-jungfrau.ch
alanrogers.com/CH9460   www.camping-jungfrau.ch

Accommodation: ☑Pitch ☑Mobile home/chalet ☐Hotel/B&B ☐Apartment

This friendly site has a very imposing and dramatic situation in a steep valley with a fine view of the Jungfrau at the end. It is a popular site and, although you should usually find space, in season do not arrive too late. A fairly extensive area with grass pitches and hardcore access roads. All 391 pitches (250 for touring) have shade in parts, electrical connections (13A) and 50 have water and drainage also. Over 30% of the pitches are taken by seasonal caravans and it is used by two tour operators. Family owned and run by Herr and Frau Fuchs, you can be sure of a warm welcome and English is spoken. You can laze here amid real mountain scenery, though it does lose the sun a little early. There are many active pursuits available in the area, as well as trips on the Jungfrau railway and mountain lifts.

You might like to know

There is a ski store on site and a free bus to ski resorts in the winter season.

- ☑ Cycling *(road)*
- ☑ Cycling *(mountain biking)*
- ☑ Sports field
- ☑ Rock climbing
- ☑ Hiking
- ☑ Skiing *(downhill)*
- ☑ Skiing *(cross-country)*
- ☑ Snowboarding
- ☑ Aerial walkways
- ☑ Ice skating

Facilities: Three fully equipped modern sanitary blocks can be heated in winter and one provides facilities for disabled visitors. Baby baths. Laundry facilities. Motorcaravan services. Well equipped campers' kitchen. Excellent shop with photo printing facility. Self-service restaurant with takeaway (May-end Oct). General room with tables and chairs, TV, drink machines, amusements. Playgrounds and covered play area. Excursions and some entertainment in high season. Mountain bike hire. Internet point and WiFi. ATM. Drying room. Ski store. Off site: Free bus to ski station (in winter only).

Open: All year.

Directions: Go through Lauterbrunnen and fork right at far end (look for signpost) before road bends left, 100 m. before church. The final approach is not very wide.
GPS: 46.58807, 7.91077

Charges guide

Per person	CHF 9,80 - 11,90
child (6-15 yrs)	CHF 4,80 - 5,50
pitch incl. electricity (plus meter in winter)	CHF 17,00 - 29,50
dog	CHF 3,00

SWITZERLAND – Engelberg

Camping Eienwäldli

Wasserfallstrasse 108, CH-6390 Engelberg (Unterwalden)
t: 041 637 1949 e: info@eienwaeldli.ch
alanrogers.com/CH9570 www.eienwaeldli.ch

Accommodation: ☑Pitch ☑Mobile home/chalet ☑Hotel/B&B ☐Apartment

This super site has facilities which must make it one of the best in Switzerland. It is situated in a beautiful location 3,500 feet above sea level, surrounded by mountains on the edge of the delightful village of Engelberg. Half of the site is taken up by static caravans which are grouped together at one side. The camping area is in two parts – nearest the entrance there are 57 hardstandings for caravans and motorcaravans, all with electricity (metered) and beyond this is a flat meadow for about 70 tents. Reception can be found in the very modern foyer of the Eienwäldli Hotel which also houses the indoor pool, health complex, shop and café/bar. The indoor pool has been most imaginatively rebuilt as a Felsenbad spa bath with adventure pool, steam and relaxing grottoes, Kneipp's cure, children's pool with water slides, solarium, Finnish sauna and eucalyptus steam bath (charged for). Being about 35 km. from Luzern by road and with a rail link, it makes a quiet, peaceful base from which to explore the Vierwaldstattersee region, walk in the mountains or just enjoy the scenery. The area is famous as a winter sports region and summer tourist resort.

You might like to know

The wellness area extends over 1,000 sq.m. on three separate floors.

- ☑ **Riding**
- ☑ **Cycling** (road)
- ☑ **Cycling** (mountain biking)
- ☑ **Sports field**
- ☑ **Golf**
- ☑ **Rock climbing**
- ☑ **Hiking**
- ☑ **Skiing** (downhill)
- ☑ **Skiing** (cross-country)

Facilities: The main toilet block, heated in cool weather, is situated at the rear of the hotel and has free hot water in washbasins (in cabins) and (charged) showers. A new modern toilet block has been added near the top end of the site. Washing machines and dryers. Shop. Café/bar. Small lounge. Indoor pool complex. Ski facilities including a drying room. Large play area with a rafting pool fed by fresh water from the mountain stream. Torches useful. TV. WiFi. Golf. Off site: Golf driving range and 18-hole course. Fishing and bicycle hire 1 km. Riding 2 km.

Open: All year.

Directions: From N2 Gotthard motorway, leave at exit 33 Stans-Sud and follow signs to Engelberg. Turn right at T-junction on edge of town and follow signs to 'Wasserfall' and site. GPS: 46.80940, 8.42367

Charges guide

Per person	CHF 6,00 - 9,00
child (6-15 yrs)	CHF 3,00 - 4,50
pitch incl. electricity (plus meter)	CHF 10,00 - 17,00
dog	CHF 1,30 - 2,00

Credit cards accepted (surcharge).

Camping Campofelice

Via alle Brere 7, CH-6598 Tenero (Ticino)
t: **091 745 1417** e: **camping@campofelice.ch**
alanrogers.com/CH9890 www.campofelice.ch

Accommodation: ☑Pitch ☑Mobile home/chalet ☐Hotel/B&B ☐Apartment

The largest site in Switzerland, it is bordered on the front by Lake Maggiore and on one side by the Verzasca estuary, where the site has its own marina. Campofelice is divided into rows, with 860 generously sized, individual pitches on flat grass on either side of hard access roads. Mostly well shaded, all pitches have 10/13A electricity connections and 409 also have water, drainage and TV connections. Pitches near the lake cost more (these are not available for motorcaravans until September) and a special area is reserved for small tents. The sheer quality of this superb site justifies the higher than average prices. Sporting facilities are good and there are cycle paths in the area, including into Locarno. The beach by the lake is sandy, long and wider than the usual lakeside ones. It shelves gently so that bathing is safe for children. Within a demarcated area are floating trampolines and rafts, and a specially marked section for toddlers.

You might like to know
There is a great sandy lakeside beach, ideal for beach volleyball.

☑ **Riding**
☑ **Tennis**
☑ **Cycling** (road)
☑ **Sports field**
☑ **Windsurfing**
☑ **Waterskiing**
☑ **Golf**
☑ **Canoeing**
☑ **Fishing**
☑ **Minigolf**

Facilities: The six toilet blocks (three heated) are of exemplary quality. Washing machines and dryers. Motorcaravan services. Gas supplies. Supermarket, restaurant, bar and takeaway (all season). Snack kiosk at beach. Lifeguards on duty. Tennis. Minigolf. Bicycle hire. Canoe and pedalo hire. Boat launching. Playgrounds. Doctor calls. Dogs are not accepted. New chalet for disabled visitors. Camping accessories shop. Car hire. Car wash. WiFi (charged). Off site: Fishing 500 m. Water-skiing and windsurfing 1 km. Riding 5 km. Golf 8 km. Boatyard with maintenance facilities.

Open: 22 March - 31 October.

Directions: On road 13 (Bellinzona-Locarno) take exit for Tenero. Site is signed at roundabout. Coming from the south, enter Tenero and follow signs to site. GPS: 46.168611, 8.855556

Charges guide

Per unit incl. 2 persons and electricity	CHF 38,00 - 82,00
extra person	CHF 8,00 - 11,00

FRANCE – Orpierre

Camping des Princes d'Orange

F-05700 Orpierre (Hautes-Alpes)
t: 04 92 66 22 53 e: campingorpierre@wanadoo.fr
alanrogers.com/FR05000 www.campingorpierre.com

Accommodation: ☑ Pitch ☑ Mobile home/chalet ☐ Hotel/B&B ☐ Apartment

This attractive, terraced site, set on a hillside above the village has been thoughtfully developed. Muriel, the owner, speaks excellent English and the genuine, friendly welcome means many families return year upon year, bringing in turn new generations. Divided into five terraces, each with its own toilet block, some of its 100 generously sized pitches (96 for touring) enjoy good shade from trees and have electricity connections (10A). In high season, one terrace is reserved as a one-star camping area for young people. Orpierre has an enchanting maze of medieval streets and houses, almost like a trip back through the centuries. Whether you choose to drive, climb, walk or cycle, there is plenty of wonderful scenery to discover in the immediate vicinity, whilst not far away, some exhilarating hang-gliding and parascending can be enjoyed. It is renowned as a world class rock climbing venue, with over 600 climbing routes in the surrounding mountains. For those seeking to 'get away from it all' in an area of outstanding natural beauty, there can be few more tranquil sites.

You might like to know
The medieval village of Orpierre is surrounded by towering cliffs with over 500 possible climbs at all levels.

☑ Riding
☑ Pony trekking
☑ Cycling (road)
☑ Cycling (mountain biking)
☑ Outdoor pool
☑ Rafting
☑ Canyoning
☑ Rock climbing
☑ Aerial walkways
☑ Fishing

Facilities: Six well equipped toilet blocks. Baby bath. Laundry facilities. Bread. Bar (1/4-31/10). Heated swimming pool, paddling pool (15/6-15/9). Play area with inflatable climbing tower. Boules. Games room. Fridge hire. Only gas barbecues are permitted. Free WiFi around reception area. Off site: Orpierre with a few shops and bicycle hire 500 m. Fishing 7 km. Nearest shopping centre Laragne 12 km. Riding 19 km. Hang-gliding. Parascending. Rock climbing. Walking. Mountain biking. Gorges de Guil.

Open: 1 April - 31 October.

Directions: Turn off N75 road at Eyguians onto the D30. Site is signed on left at crossroads in the centre of Orpièrre village.
GPS: 44.31121, 5.69677

Charges guide

Per unit incl. 2 persons and electricity	€ 21,10 - € 27,70
extra person	€ 5,50 - € 7,80
child (under 7 yrs)	€ 3,00 - € 3,70
dog	€ 1,70

No credit cards.

Domaine le Pommier

RN 102, F-07170 Villeneuve-de-Berg (Ardèche)
t: **04 75 94 82 81** e: **info@campinglepommier.com**
alanrogers.com/FR07110 www.campinglepommier.com

Accommodation: ☑Pitch ☑Mobile home/chalet ☐Hotel/B&B ☐Apartment

Domaine le Pommier is an extremely spacious, Dutch owned site of 10 hectares in 32 hectares of wooded grounds centred around a spectacular pirate themed water park. The site is steeply terraced and has wonderful views over the Ardèche mountains and beyond. There are 611 pitches, with 275 for touring units, the rest used for mobile homes and chalets for rent. They are on sandy grass, of a good size and well spaced. Separated by trees and hedges, some have less shade. All have access to electricity and water is close by. The site is not recommended for very large units. The site has first class facilities. These include the most up-to-date toilet blocks, a very good bar/restaurant and one of the best pirate themed swimming and paddling pool complexes we have seen, with amazing water slides with varying levels of thrill and excitement – ideal for all the family. The poolside catering is good and this area could keep you occupied all day with loungers available for relaxation before returning to the delights in Buccaneer Bay! The entertainment programme provided throughout the day and into the evening is comprehensive and for all ages.

You might like to know
The site is just 1,500 m. (at an altitude of 300 m!) from Villeneuve-de-Berg with its 2,500 inhabitants. The village was founded in 1284 and became famous for the cultivation of mulberry trees for silk production.

- ☑ **Cycling** *(mountain biking)*
- ☑ **Sports field**
- ☑ **Archery**
- ☑ **Canyoning**
- ☑ **Potholing**
- ☑ **Rock climbing**
- ☑ **Hiking**
- ☑ **Canoeing**
- ☑ **Water games**
- ☑ **Orienteering**

Facilities: Four excellent toilet blocks, one with underfloor heating, provide all the necessary facilities. Comprehensive shop. Bar/restaurant. Swimming pool complex with exciting slides, paddling pools, etc. Everything opens all season. Boules. Minigolf. Large multisports area. Activities including games in the woods, archery, water polo and tug-of-war. Watercolour classes. Tennis. Soundproofed disco. Very extensive programme of events on and off site. Low season excursions. Entertainment programme exclusively in Dutch. WiFi (charged). Off site: Villeneuve-de-Berg 1.5 km. River Ardèche 12 km. Potholing, rock climbing, canoeing, canyoning, mountain biking, walking and riding.

Open: 21 April - 15 September.

Directions: Site is west of Montélimar on the N102. The entrance is adjacent to the roundabout at the eastern end of the Villeneuve-de-Berg bypass. GPS: 44.57250, 4.51115

Charges guide

Per unit incl. 2 persons and electricity	€ 23,50 - € 43,50
extra person	€ 5,50 - € 9,50
child (4-12 yrs)	€ 3,50 - € 6,50
dog	free - € 4,50

Castel Nature Parc l'Ardéchois

Route touristique des Gorges, F-07150 Vallon-Pont-d'Arc (Ardèche)
t: 04 75 88 06 63   e: ardecamp@bigfoot.com
alanrogers.com/FR07120   www.ardechois-camping.com

Accommodation: ☑Pitch   ☑Mobile home/chalet   ☐ Hotel/B&B   ☐Apartment

This very high quality, family run site is within walking distance of Vallon-Pont-d'Arc.
It borders the River Ardèche and canoe trips are run, professionally, direct from the
site. This campsite is ideal for families with younger children seeking an active holiday.
The facilities are comprehensive and the central toilet unit is of an extremely high
standard. Of the 244 pitches, there are 225 for touring units, separated by trees and
individual shrubs. All have electrical connections (6/10A) and 125 have full services.
Forming a focal point are the bar and restaurant (good menus), with a terrace and
stage overlooking the attractive heated pool. There is also a large paddling pool and
sunbathing terrace. For children, there is a well thought out play area plus plenty of
other space for youngsters to play, both on the site and along the river. Activities are
organised throughout the season; these are family based – no discos. Patrols at night
ensure a good night's sleep. Access to the site is easy and suitable for large outfits. The
campsite is ideally situated near the Pont-d'Arc, a huge arch of limestone in the Ardèche
Gorge. Member of Leading Campings Group.

You might like to know

The River Ardèche offers a range of leisure
activities, whether you want to relax on the
shore, take a cooling dip in the gurgling
waters or take to the rapids in a canoe.

- ☑ Riding
- ☑ Pony trekking
- ☑ Tennis
- ☑ Cycling (road)
- ☑ Cycling (mountain biking)
- ☑ Sports field
- ☑ Outdoor pool
- ☑ Crafts
- ☑ Paintball
- ☑ Rafting

- ☑ Canyoning
- ☑ Potholing
- ☑ Rock climbing
- ☑ Hiking
- ☑ Aerial walkways

Facilities: Two well equipped toilet blocks, one
superb with everything working automatically.
Facilities are of the highest standard, very clean
and include good facilities for babies, those with
disabilities, washing up and laundry. Four private
bathrooms to hire. Washing machines. Well
stocked shop. Swimming pool and paddling pool
(no Bermuda shorts). Massage and gym. Tennis.
Very good play area. Internet access. Organised
activities, canoe trips. Only gas barbecues are
permitted. Communal barbecue area. WiFi
(charged). Off site: Canoeing, rafting, walking,
riding, mountain biking, golf, rock climbing,
bowling, wine tasting and dining. Vallon-Pont-
d'Arc 800 m. Explore the real Ardèche on the
minor roads and visit Labaume, Balazuc and
Largentière (market Tuesday).

Open: 1 April - 30 September.

Directions: From Vallon-Pont-d'Arc (western end
of the Ardèche Gorge) at a roundabout go east
on the D290. Site entrance is shortly on the right.
GPS: 44.39804, 4.39878

Charges guide

Per unit incl. 2 persons and electricity	€ 26,00 - € 58,00
extra person	€ 6,00 - € 10,00
child (0-13 yrs)	€ 4,30 - € 7,90

Camping l'Arize

Lieu-dit Bourtol, F-09240 La Bastide-de-Sérou (Ariège)
t: 05 61 65 81 51   e: mail@camping-arize.com
alanrogers.com/FR09020   www.camping-arize.com

Accommodation: ☑Pitch ☑Mobile home/chalet ☐Hotel/B&B ☐Apartment

The site sits in a delightful, tranquil valley among the foothills of the Pyrenees and is just east of the interesting village of La Bastide-de-Sérou beside the River Arize (good trout fishing). The river is fenced for the safety of children on the site, but may be accessed just outside the gate. The 71 large touring pitches are neatly laid out on level grass within the spacious site. All have 6/10A electricity and are mostly separated into bays by hedges and young trees. Full services are available to some pitches with access to a small toilet block. You will receive a warm welcome from Dominique and Brigitte at this friendly little family site, and Brigitte speaks excellent English. Discounts have been negotiated for several of the local attractions (details are provided in the comprehensive pack provided on arrival – in your own language). This is a comfortable and relaxing base for touring this beautiful part of the Pyrenees within easy reach of the medieval town of Foix, and Andorra for duty-free shopping. Deer and wild boar are common in this area and may be sighted in quieter periods. Walking and cycling maps are available.

You might like to know
There are over 100 km. of waymarked trails within easy reach of the site.

- ☑ Riding
- ☑ Pony trekking
- ☑ Tennis
- ☑ Cycling *(road)*
- ☑ Cycling *(mountain biking)*
- ☑ Outdoor pool
- ☑ Golf
- ☑ Paintball
- ☑ Rafting
- ☑ Hiking
- ☑ Kayaking
- ☑ Fitness/gym
- ☑ 10-pin bowling
- ☑ Fishing

Facilities: Toilet block includes facilities for babies and disabled visitors. Laundry room. Motorcaravan services. Shop. Small swimming pool and sunbathing area. Entertainment in high season. Weekly barbecues and welcome drinks on Sundays. Fishing. Bicycle hire. WiFi (charged). Off site: Several restaurants and shops within a few minutes drive. The nearest restaurant is located at the national stud for the famous Merens horses just 200 m. away and will deliver takeaway meals to your pitch. Golf 5 km.

Open: 9 March - 10 November.

Directions: Site is southeast of the village of La Bastide-de-Sérou. Take the D15 towards Nescus and site is on right after 1 km. GPS: 43.00182, 1.44538

Charges guide

Per unit incl. 2 persons and electricity	€ 17,40 - € 29,60
extra person	€ 4,20 - € 6,30
child (7-13 yrs)	€ 3,80 - € 4,90
dog	€ 1,20 - € 2,20

FRANCE – Narbonne

Yelloh! Village les Mimosas

Chaussée de Mandirac, F-11100 Narbonne (Aude)
t: 04 68 49 03 72 e: info@lesmimosas.com
alanrogers.com/FR11070 www.lesmimosas.com

Accommodation: ☑Pitch ☑Mobile home/chalet ☐ Hotel/B&B ☐Apartment

Six kilometres inland from the beaches of Narbonne and Gruissan, this site benefits from a less hectic situation than others by the sea. The site is lively with plenty to amuse and entertain the younger generation whilst offering facilities for the whole family. A free club card is available in July/August for use of the children's club, gym, sauna, tennis, minigolf, billiards etc. There are 250 pitches, 150 for touring, many in a circular layout, and of a very good size, most with 6A electricity. There are a few 'grand confort' pitches with reasonable shade, mostly from two-metre high hedges. There are also a number of mobile homes and chalets to rent. This could be a very useful site offering many possibilities to meet a variety of needs, on-site entertainment (including an evening on Cathar history), and easy access to popular beaches. Nearby Gruissan is a fascinating village with its wooden houses on stilts, beaches, ruined castle, port and salt beds. Narbonne has Roman remains and inland Cathar castles are to be found perched on rugged hill tops.

You might like to know
Discover the charms of the Mediterranean. Tennis, fishing, riding, hiking, cycling, mountain biking, sailing, golf and creative crafts are just some of the activities available.

- ☑ Pony trekking
- ☑ Surfing
- ☑ Windsurfing
- ☑ Kitesurfing
- ☑ Diving
- ☑ Waterskiing
- ☑ Paintball
- ☑ Canoeing
- ☑ Go-karting
- ☑ 10-pin bowling

Facilities: Sanitary buildings refurbished to a high standard include a baby room. Washing machines. Shop and Auberge restaurant (open all season). Takeaway. Bar. Small lounge, amusements (July/Aug). Landscaped heated pool with slides and islands (open 1/5), plus the original pool and children's pool (high season). Play area. Minigolf. Mountain bike hire. Tennis. Sauna and new gym. Children's activities, sports, entertainment (high season). Bicycle hire. Multisports ground. WiFi. Off site: Lagoon with boating and fishing via footpath 200 m. Riding and windsurfing/sailing school 300 m. Gruissan's beach 10 minutes.

Open: 28 March - 1 November.

Directions: From A9 exit 38 (Narbonne Sud) take last exit on roundabout, back over the autoroute (site signed from here). Follow signs for La Nautique and then Mandirac and site (6 km. from autoroute). Also signed from Narbonne centre. GPS: 43.13662, 3.02562

Charges guide

Per unit incl. 2 persons and electricity	€ 17,50 - € 36,00
extra person	€ 4,10 - € 8,00
child (2-7 yrs)	free - € 6,00
dog	€ 1,50 - € 3,50

FRANCE – Locunolé

Castel Camping le Ty-Nadan

Route d'Arzano, F-29310 Locunolé (Finistère)
t: **02 98 71 75 47** e: **info@camping-ty-nadan.fr**
alanrogers.com/FR29010 www.camping-ty-nadan.fr

Accommodation: ☑Pitch ☑Mobile home/chalet ☐Hotel/B&B ☐Apartment

Camping le Ty-Nadan is a well organised site set amongst wooded countryside along the bank of the River Elle. There are 183 grassy pitches for touring units, many with shade and 99 fully serviced. The pool complex with slides and paddling pool is very popular as are the large indoor pool complex and indoor games area with a climbing wall. There is also an adventure play park and a play park for 5-8 year olds, not to mention tennis courts, table tennis, pool tables, archery and trampolines. New 'floating' accommodation on the lake was opened in 2012. This is a wonderful site for families with children. Several tour operators use the site. An exciting and varied programme of activities is offered throughout the season – canoeing and sea kayaking expeditions, rock climbing, mountain biking, aquagym, paintball, riding and walking – all supervised by qualified staff. A full programme of entertainment for all ages is provided in high season, including concerts, Breton evenings with hog roasts, dancing, etc. (be warned, you will be actively encouraged to join in!).

You might like to know
All the on-site activities are led by fully qualified staff. There are plenty of opportunities too for fishing, cycling and mountain biking.

- ☑ Riding
- ☑ Pony trekking
- ☑ Tennis
- ☑ Archery
- ☑ Paintball
- ☑ Rock climbing
- ☑ Zip wires
- ☑ Canoeing
- ☑ Kayaking
- ☑ Climbing wall
- ☑ Adventure park
- ☑ Quad bikes

Facilities: One new, split-level toilet block is of good quality and includes washbasins in cabins and baby rooms. Two other blocks provide easier access for disabled campers. Washing machines and dryers. Restaurant, takeaway, bar and well stocked shop. Heated outdoor pool (17x8 m). Indoor pool. Small river beach (unfenced). Indoor badminton and rock climbing facility. Activity and entertainment programmes (all season). Riding centre. Bicycle hire. Boat hire. Canoe trips. Fishing. Internet access and WiFi (charged). Off site: Beaches 20 minutes by car. Golf 12 km.

Open: 20 April - 2 September.

Directions: Make for Arzano which is northeast of Quimperlé on the Pontivy road and turn off D22 just west of village at site sign. Site is 3 km. GPS: 47.90468, -3.47477

Charges guide

Per unit incl. 2 persons and electricity	€ 19,80 - € 50,40
extra person	€ 4,30 - € 8,80
child (2-6 yrs)	€ 2,00 - € 5,40
dog	€ 2,10 - € 5,80

Camping de la Torche

Pointe de la Roche, F-29120 Plomeur-la Torche (Finistère)
t: **02 98 58 62 82** e: **info@campingdelatorche.fr**
alanrogers.com/FR29370 www.campingdelatorche.fr

Accommodation: ☑Pitch ☑Mobile home/chalet   ☐Hotel/B&B ☐Apartment

Probably a 'must stay' site for surfers, this rural, family owned, wooded campsite, like so many in this part of Brittany, comes to life in July and August. The natural beauty of the wide sandy beaches of la Torche can be accessed direct from the site via a footpath (1.5 km). La Torche is internationally renowned as a paradise for all boardsports, particularly windsurfing. The site has 155 pitches (115 for tourers), divided by trees and hedges and tending to the generous in size. Around 40 chalets and mobile homes are discreetly positioned amongst the trees. After an energetic or a relaxing day on the beach, you can enjoy a drink at the bar or on the terrace overlooking the site's pool. There is one modern toilet block of a very good standard. Provisions are available at a supermarket in Plomeur (3 km).

You might like to know

The beach is within walking distance and there is a range of watersports – surfing, kite-surfing, windboarding etc. There are aeromodelism shows in summer.

- ☑ Riding
- ☑ Pony trekking
- ☑ Cycling (road)
- ☑ Cycling (mountain biking)
- ☑ Sports field
- ☑ Outdoor pool
- ☑ Crafts
- ☑ Sailing
- ☑ Surfing
- ☑ Windsurfing

- ☑ Kitesurfing
- ☑ Diving
- ☑ Waterskiing
- ☑ Hiking
- ☑ Aerial walkways

Facilities: The main (heated) toilet block provides British style toilets, showers, washing cubicles and good facilities for disabled visitors. A second block opens in high season. Washing machine and dryers. Shop, bar and terrace, with snacks (all 1/7-31/8). Covered swimming pool (15/6-15/9). Play area. Games/TV room. Entertainment in July/Aug. Free WiFi in bar. Off site: Riding 500 m. Beach and fishing 1.5 km. Shops in Plomeur 3 km.

Open: 1 April - 23 September.

Directions: From Pont l'Abbé the D785 south to Plomeur, then follow signs for Pointe de La Torche. After 3 km. site is signed to left. GPS: 47.832859, -4.326355

Charges guide

Per unit incl. 2 persons	
and electricity	€ 17,10 - € 23,40
extra person	€ 3,50 - € 4,90
child (0-7 yrs)	€ 2,20 - € 3,00
dog	free - € 2,00

Airotel Camping de la Côte d'Argent

F-33990 Hourtin-Plage (Gironde)
t: **05 56 09 10 25** e: **info@cca33.com**
alanrogers.com/FR33110 www.cca33.com

Accommodation: ☑Pitch ☑Mobile home/chalet ☑Hotel/B&B ☐Apartment

Côte d'Argent is a large, well equipped site for leisurely family holidays. It makes an ideal base for walkers and cyclists with over 100 km. of cycle lanes in the area. Hourtin-Plage is a pleasant invigorating resort on the Atlantic coast and a popular location for watersports enthusiasts. The site's top attraction is its pool complex, where wooden bridges connect the pools and islands, and there are sunbathing and play areas plus an indoor heated pool. The site has 600 touring pitches (all with 10A electricity), not always clearly defined, arranged under trees with some on sand. High quality entertainment takes place at the impressive bar/restaurant near the entrance. Spread over 20 hectares of undulating sand-based terrain and in the midst of a pine forest. The site is well organised and ideal for children.

You might like to know

There is plenty to occupy visitors – the large aquatic complex (3,500 sq.m) with covered, heated pool, a multisports court and the Activity Centre with shops, games room, bicycle hire, video games and fitness room.

- ☑ Riding
- ☑ Pony trekking
- ☑ Tennis
- ☑ Cycling *(road)*
- ☑ Cycling *(mountain biking)*
- ☑ Sports field
- ☑ Outdoor pool
- ☑ Crafts
- ☑ Archery
- ☑ Sailing

- ☑ Surfing
- ☑ Kitesurfing
- ☑ Waterskiing
- ☑ Aerial walkways
- ☑ Kayaking

Facilities: Very clean sanitary blocks include provision for disabled visitors. Washing machines. Motorcaravan service points. Large supermarket, restaurant, takeaway, pizzeria, bar (all open 1/6-15/9). Four outdoor pools with slides and flumes (1/6-19/9). Indoor pool (all season). Fitness room. Massage (Institut de Beauté). Tennis. Play areas. Miniclub, organised entertainment in season. Bicycle hire. WiFi (charged). ATM. Charcoal barbecues are not permitted. Hotel (12 rooms). Off site: Path to the beach 300 m. Fishing and riding. Golf 30 km.

Open: 14 May - 18 September.

Directions: Turn off D101 Hourtin-Soulac road 3 km. north of Hourtin. Then join D101E signed Hourtin-Plage. Site is 300 m. from the beach. GPS: 45.22297, -1.16465

Charges guide

Per unit incl. 2 persons and electricity	€ 28,00 - € 53,00
extra person	€ 4,00 - € 8,50
child (3-9 yrs)	€ 3,00 - € 7,50
dog	€ 2,00 - € 6,50

Camping le Tedey

Par le Moutchic, route de Longarisse, F-33680 Lacanau-Lac (Gironde)
t: 05 56 03 00 15   e: camping@le-tedey.com
alanrogers.com/FR33290   www.le-tedey.com

Accommodation: ☑Pitch ☑Mobile home/chalet ☐Hotel/B&B ☐Apartment

With direct access to a large lake and beach, this site enjoys a beautiful tranquil position set in an area of 14 hectares amidst mature pine trees. There are 680 pitches of which 620 are for touring units, with just 38 mobile homes and chalets available for rent. The pitches are generally level and grassy although parts of the site are on a slope. The pitches are shady with dappled sunlight breaking through the trees. Electricity is available to all pitches and 213 also have water and waste water drainage. The bar is close to the lake with a large indoor and outdoor seating area. The owners and staff are friendly and helpful and English is spoken. There is an open-air cinema on Saturdays and Wednesdays as well as other entertainment in July and August. A children's club is also organised. The takeaway sells a variety of food and the shop next door is well stocked. This is an attractive, well maintained site where you get a feeling of space and calm. There are many places of interest nearby and it is a short drive from Bordeaux.

You might like to know
Why not visit the bustling city of Bordeaux? It is less than one hour away.

- ☑ Riding
- ☑ Cycling (road)
- ☑ Cycling (mountain biking)
- ☑ Sailing
- ☑ Windsurfing
- ☑ Golf
- ☑ Hiking
- ☑ Canoeing
- ☑ Pedaloes
- ☑ Fishing

Facilities: Four modern sanitary blocks with facilities for disabled visitors and babies. Laundry facilities. Shop (8/5-15/9). Bar with terrace (1/6-15/9). Crêperie (16/6-11/9). Takeaway (25/6-3/9). Bicycle hire. Boating on the lake. Fishing. Pétanque. Playground. Gas barbecues only. Dogs are not accepted in July/Aug. WiFi throughout (charged). Off site: Riding and golf 3 km. Beach 5 km. Surfing. Cycling.

Open: 27 April - 21 September.

Directions: From Lacanau take the D6 to Lacanau-Océan. Take Route de Longarisse and the site is well signed. GPS: 44.98620, -1.13410

Charges guide

Per unit incl. 2 persons and electricity	€ 21,00 - € 30,00

FRANCE – Portiragnes-Plage

Camping les Sablons

Avenue des Muriers, F-34420 Portiragnes-Plage (Hérault)
t: **04 67 90 90 55** e: **contact@les-sablons.com**
alanrogers.com/FR34400 www.les-sablons.com

Accommodation: ☑Pitch ☑Mobile home/chalet ☐Hotel/B&B ☐Apartment

Les Sablons is an impressive and popular site with lots going on, a village in itself. Most of the facilities are arranged around the entrance with shops, a restaurant, a bar and a large pool complex with no less than five slides and three heated pools. There is also direct access to a white sandy beach at the back of the site, close to a small lake. There is good shade on the majority of the site, although some of the newer touring pitches have less shade but are nearer the gate to the beach. On level sandy grass, all have 6A electricity. Of the 800 pitches, around half are taken by a range of mobile homes and chalets (many for hire, and a few for use by tour operators). A new entertainment office enables you to book a wide range of sporting, cultural and musical activities as well as excursions. Children's clubs and evening entertainment are organised. In fact, this is a real holiday venue aiming to keep all the family happy. Some visitors simply stay on the site for their entire holiday – it certainly has everything. The site is very convenient for Béziers airport.

You might like to know
There is a free daily activity programme organised by the campsite staff. In addition to a wide range of sports, there are arts and crafts activities such as painting and pottery.

- ☑ Riding
- ☑ Tennis
- ☑ Outdoor pool
- ☑ Crafts
- ☑ Archery
- ☑ Aerial walkways
- ☑ Zip wires
- ☑ Climbing wall
- ☑ Fitness/gym
- ☑ Go-karting

Facilities: Well equipped, modernised toilet blocks include large showers, some with washbasins. Baby baths and facilities for disabled visitors. Supermarket, bakery and newsagent. Restaurant, bar and takeaway. Swimming pool complex. Entertainment and activity programme with sports, music and cultural activities. Children's club. Beach club. Tennis. Archery. Play areas. Electronic games. ATM. Internet access. WiFi throughout site. Off site: Village and bicycle hire 100 m. Beach and riding 200 m. Canal du Midi 1 km. Parc Adventure (high wire adventure park) 1.5 km.

Open: 1 April - 30 September.

Directions: From A9 exit 35 (Béziers Est) follow signs for Vias and Agde (N112). After large roundabout pass exit to Cers then take exit for Portiragnes (D37). Follow for 5 km. and pass over Canal du Midi towards Portiragnes-Plage. Site is on left after roundabout.
GPS: 43.28003, 3.36396

Charges guide

Per unit incl. 2 persons and electricity	€ 20,00 - € 50,00
extra person	€ 6,00 - € 10,00
child (acc. to age)	free - € 10,00
dog	€ 4,00

FRANCE – Pierrefitte-sur-Sauldre

Leading Camping les Alicourts

Domaine des Alicourts, F-41300 Pierrefitte-sur-Sauldre (Loir-et-Cher)
t: 02 54 88 63 34 e: info@lesalicourts.com
alanrogers.com/FR41030 www.lesalicourts.com

Accommodation: ☑Pitch ☑Mobile home/chalet ☐ Hotel/B&B ☐Apartment

A secluded holiday village set in the heart of the forest, with many sporting facilities and a super spa centre, Camping les Alicourts is midway between Orléans and Bourges, to the east of the A71. There are 490 pitches, 150 for touring and the remainder occupied by mobile homes and chalets. All pitches have electricity connections (6A) and good provision for water, and most are 150 sq.m. (min. 100 sq.m.). Locations vary, from wooded to more open areas, thus giving a choice of amount of shade. All facilities are open all season and the leisure amenities are exceptional. The Senseo Balnéo centre offers indoor pools, hydrotherapy, massage and spa treatments for over 18s only (some special family sessions are provided). An inviting outdoor water complex (all season) includes two swimming pools, a pool with wave machine and a beach area, not forgetting three water slides. Competitions and activities are organised for adults and children, including a high season club for children with an entertainer twice a day, a disco once a week and a dance for adults. A member of Leading Campings group.

You might like to know
All activities are available from the day the site opens to the day it closes. Family activity passes are available and the Kids' Club and entertainment are free.

- ☑ Riding
- ☑ Pony trekking
- ☑ Tennis
- ☑ Cycling (road)
- ☑ Sports field
- ☑ Outdoor pool
- ☑ Archery
- ☑ Waterskiing
- ☑ Golf
- ☑ Canoeing
- ☑ Kayaking
- ☑ Pedaloes
- ☑ Fitness/gym
- ☑ Go-karting
- ☑ Fishing

Facilities: Three modern sanitary blocks include some washbasins in cabins and baby bathrooms. Laundry facilities. Facilities for disabled visitors. Motorcaravan services. Shop. Restaurant. Takeaway in bar with terrace. Pool complex. Spa centre. 7-hectare lake (fishing, bathing, canoes, pedaloes, cable-ski). 9-hole golf course. Adventure play area. Tennis. Minigolf. Boules. Roller skating/skateboarding (bring own equipment). Bicycle hire. Internet access and WiFi (charged).

Open: 27 April - 7 September.

Directions: From A71, take Lamotte-Beuvron exit (no 3) or from N20 Orléans to Vierzon turn left on to D923 towards Aubigny. After 14 km. turn right at camping sign on to D24E. Site signed in 2 km. GPS: 47.54398, 2.19193

Charges guide

Per unit incl. 2 persons and electricity	€ 20,00 - € 46,00
extra person	€ 7,00 - € 10,00
child (1-17 yrs acc. to age)	free - € 9,00
dog	€ 5,00 - € 7,00

Camping Soleil du Pibeste

16 avenue du Lavedan, F-65400 Agos-Vidalos (Hautes-Pyrénées)
t: **05 62 97 53 23** e: **info@campingpibeste.com**
alanrogers.com/FR65090 www.campingpibeste.com

Accommodation: ☑Pitch ☑Mobile home/chalet ☐ Hotel/B&B ☐Apartment

The Dusserm family, the owners, are very proud of their regional culture and heritage and will ensure you are made welcome. The reception is friendly, with an area for local foods, maps and good tourist information. This site is special because of the range and type of activities that it offers. These include tai chi, qi gong, massage, archery, walking, climbing and canoeing. Choral and creative activities are offered. There are 38 touring pitches all with 3-15A electricity. Mobile homes and chalets are available to rent. The mountain view from the terrace is magnificent. Ongoing improvements include a second swimming pool incorporating facilities for campers with disabilities. Play areas are being expanded to cater for different age groups, including lively teenagers. There is a shop and bread can be ordered for delivery the following morning. The bar and restaurant area is large and well equipped. The site is rural but has a bus stop just outside providing access to Argelès-Gazost and the renowned pilgrimage town of Lourdes. The family also offers a pick up service from various airports and towns.

You might like to know

A variety of courses are on offer, with qualified instructors.

- ☑ Riding
- ☑ Pony trekking
- ☑ Tennis
- ☑ Outdoor pool
- ☑ Crafts
- ☑ Archery
- ☑ Paintball
- ☑ Rafting
- ☑ Canyoning
- ☑ Potholing
- ☑ Zip wires
- ☑ Canoeing
- ☑ Kayaking
- ☑ Climbing wall
- ☑ Fishing

Facilities: Two heated toilet blocks. Baby room. Facilities for disabled visitors (key). Cleaning can be variable. Washing machine, dryer. Motorcaravan services. Bar, snack bar, restaurant and pizzeria (June-Sept). Shop for essentials. Bread can be ordered for next day delivery. Swimming pool with panoramic views and loungers (June-Sept). New children's play areas (4-6 yrs and 6-10 yrs). Multisports pitch. Volleyball. Tennis. Badminton. Bowling. Basketball. 4 free activities weekly (tai chi, qi gong, rollerblading, archery, etc; July/Aug). Entertainment programme, children's activities and craft workshops (July/Aug). Massage (charged). Library. WiFi (charged).
Off site: Fishing 800 m. Rafting 2 km. Golf 10 km. Riding 15 km. Skiing 20 km.

Open: 1 May - 30 September.

Directions: Agos Vidalos is on the N21, which becomes the D821, 5 km. south of Lourdes. Leave expressway at second exit, signed Agos Vidalos and continue on D921B to site, a short distance on the right. GPS: 43.03557, -0.07093

Charges guide

Per unit incl. 2 persons and electricity	€ 25,00 - € 34,00
extra person	€ 8,00

Sunêlia les Tropiques

Boulevard de la plage, F-66440 Torreilles-Plage (Pyrénées-Orientales)
t: 04 68 28 05 09 e: contact@campinglestropiques.com
alanrogers.com/FR66190 www.campinglestropiques.com

Accommodation: ☑Pitch ☑Mobile home/chalet ☐ Hotel/B&B ☐Apartment

Les Tropiques is a very attractive site with a large pool complex, only 400 metres from a sandy beach. It will provide families with children of all ages with an ideal seaside holiday. There are 450 pitches with 78 for touring units, all with 6/10A electricity. Pleasant pine and palm trees with other Mediterranean vegetation give shade and provide a pleasant environment. Activities are provided for all including a large range of sports, activities, cabarets and shows. The pool complex at les Tropiques is very impressive with four pools, two heated with good provision for children, including a range of toboggans, all surrounded by spacious sunbathing terraces with loungers and parasols. Two play areas are provided – one for smaller children, the other with bridges and slides for the older ones. A wellness centre was due to open just after we visited.

You might like to know

The site is just 400 m. from the sea, with 3,200 sq.m. of water space, swimming pools, slides and childrens aqua playground. New for 2013 – spa wellness with hammam and jacuzzi. All ideally situated for discovering the beautiful Catalan countryside.

- ☑ Riding
- ☑ Tennis
- ☑ Cycling (mountain biking)
- ☑ Sports field
- ☑ Outdoor pool
- ☑ Archery
- ☑ Sailing
- ☑ Diving
- ☑ Waterskiing
- ☑ Paintball

- ☑ Fitness/gym
- ☑ Go-karting
- ☑ Fishing
- ☑ Aquagym
- ☑ Water polo

Facilities: Modern, fully equipped sanitary facilities, provision for disabled visitors. Launderette. Shop (7/4-30/9). Bar and Restaurant (15/5-15/9). Takeaway and pizzeria (1/7-31/8). Heated pool (all season) and water slides. Paddling pool. Wellness centre. Outdoor fitness equipment. Tennis (floodlit). Multisports area (basketball, football, volleyball). Pétanque. Archery (1/7-31/8). TV/billiards room. Play area. Disco (every evening). Miniclub (6-12 yrs; July/Aug). Bicycle hire (15/6-15/9). WiFi over site (charged). Off site: Minigolf 300 m. Riding, windsurf board hire and sea fishing 400 m. Microlights, karting 1.5 km. Diving, waterskiing 4 km. Golf 15 km.

Open: 7 April - 30 September.

Directions: From A9 exit Perpignan Nord, follow D83 towards Le Barcarès for 9 km. Take D81 south towards Canet for 3 km. turn left at roundabout for Torreilles-Plage. Site is the last but one on left. GPS: 42.7675, 3.02972

Charges guide

Per unit incl. 2 persons and electricity	€ 18,00 - € 48,50
extra person	€ 3,85 - € 9,20
child (0-13 yrs)	€ 2,55 - € 7,15
dog	€ 4,00

FRANCE – Le Barcarès

Camping le Floride et l'Embouchure

Route de Saint Laurent, F-66423 Le Barcarès (Pyrénées-Orientales)
t: **04 68 86 11 75** e: **campingfloride@aol.com**
alanrogers.com/FR66290 www.floride.fr

Accommodation: ☑Pitch ☑Mobile home/chalet ☐ Hotel/B&B ☐Apartment

Essentially a family run enterprise, le Floride et l'Embouchure is really two sites in one – l'Embouchure the smaller one with direct access to the beach and le Floride on the opposite side of the road into Le Barcarès village. There are a number of pitches with their own individual sanitary facility and in total the site offers 632 reasonably sized pitches, 280 for touring, all with 10A electricity. A good range of chalets and mobile homes are available for rent. This is a very friendly family-centred site, very popular with Dutch visitors. It is relatively inexpensive, especially outside the July/August peak period. There is an excellent aquapark at le Floride with a number of water slides and a covered pool. The busy town of Le Barcarès is within easy walking distance. The Voie Vert cycleway runs alongside the river Agly which borders l'Embouchure (the river has high banks so it is not seen from the site). There is a purpose-built cycleway from Le Barcarès to Rivesaltes.

You might like to know
The site has direct access to the sea (100 m) and to a 3,000 sq.m. aquatic complex with a covered, heated swimming pool, a paddling pool with games, a jacuzzi and fun slides.

- ☑ Riding
- ☑ Pony trekking
- ☑ Tennis
- ☑ Cycling (road)
- ☑ Cycling (mountain biking)
- ☑ Sports field
- ☑ Outdoor pool
- ☑ Crafts
- ☑ Sailing
- ☑ Surfing
- ☑ Windsurfing
- ☑ Kitesurfing
- ☑ Diving
- ☑ Waterskiing
- ☑ Paintball

Facilities: Four fully equipped toilet blocks on le Floride and two on l'Embouchure where 50 pitches near the beach have individual facilities. Facilities for babies and disabled visitors. Family shower room. Motorcaravan service point. Shop, bar, restaurant and takeaway (all 15/6-5/9). Pool complex (all season). Excellent play area. Multisports court. Gym. Tennis. Entertainment and sports programmes (mid June-mid Sept). Bicycle hire. Charcoal barbecues are not permitted. Max. 1 dog. WiFi throughout (charged). Off site: Beach 100 m. Fishing 1 km. Riding 1.5 km.

Open: 1 April - 30 September.

Directions: From A9 take exit 41 (Perpignan Nord) and follow signs for Canet and Le Barcarès via D83. At J9 follow D81 (Canet) then next left into Le Barcarès Village. Site is 1 km. on the left and right sides of the road.
GPS: 42.77855, 3.0301

Charges guide

Per unit incl. 2 persons and electricity	€ 12,50 - € 34,00
incl. private sanitary facility	€ 16,00 - € 42,00
extra person	€ 2,60 - € 6,20
child (1-4 yrs)	free - € 3,60

Camping le Lamparo

Route de la Plage, F-66470 Sainte Marie-la-Mer (Pyrénées-Orientales)
t: **04 68 73 83 87** e: **info@campinglamparo.com**
alanrogers.com/FR66450 www.campinglamparo.com

Accommodation: ☑Pitch ☑Mobile home/chalet ☐ Hotel/B&B ☐Apartment

A small, family run site of just 156 pitches, le Lamparo is hidden away on the edge of Sainte Marie-le-Mer. M. and Mme. Fischer, the owners, have created an environment for a good family holiday without all the noise and distractions that can often be found on larger sites. Large flat pitches provide ample space and there are differing degrees of shade and screening to suit most preferences. There is plenty to do on site, so no need to drive out in search of activities, and you can take advantage of the close proximity to both Sainte Marie town and the beach. There is a selection of accommodation to rent on site ranging from two person caravans to mobile homes for up to six people. There are also bungalows, which are very strong reinforced vinyl square tents on concrete bases, for four people.

You might like to know
There's plenty of activity in the swimming pool, including a regular aqua gym.

- ☑ Tennis
- ☑ Cycling *(road)*
- ☑ Outdoor pool
- ☑ Crafts
- ☑ Windsurfing
- ☑ Waterskiing
- ☑ Golf
- ☑ Hiking
- ☑ Fitness/gym
- ☑ Fishing

Facilities: Two good toilet blocks are bright with an open design, with some washbasins in cabins. Dedicated facilities for babies and disabled visitors. Washing machines. Basic provisions from the bar (shops nearby). Bar and restaurant with takeaway. Good sized swimming pool. Jacuzzi, sauna and gym. Indoor games area. Outdoor sports facilities. Tennis. Small play area. Activities for young children in high season. WiFi over site (charged). Off site: Resort facilities within 1.2 km. as well as the small town of Sainte Marie. Riding, fishing, watersports and amusement parks all within 10 minutes drive.

Open: All year.

Directions: Leave A9 at exit 41 and take the D83 towards St Laurent. Turn right on D81 and head south towards Sainte Marie. Site is signed at the roundabout. GPS: 42.72841, 3.02477

Charges guide

Per unit incl. 2 persons and electricity	€ 12,00 - € 29,00
extra person	€ 3,00 - € 7,00
child (under 4 yrs)	free - € 2,00
dog	free - € 4,00

FRANCE – Argelès-sur-Mer

Camping la Sirène

Route de Taxo à la Mer, F-66702 Argelès-sur-Mer (Pyrénées-Orientales)
t: 04 68 81 04 61 e: contact@camping-lasirene.fr
alanrogers.com/FR66560 www.camping-lasirene.fr

Accommodation: ☑Pitch ☑Mobile home/chalet ☐Hotel/B&B ☐Apartment

From the moment you step into the hotel-like reception area you realise that this large site offers the holiday maker everything they could want, including a super pool complex, in a well managed and convenient location close to Argelès-sur-Mer and the beaches. There are 740 pitches over the 17-hectare site, and 520 mobile homes and chalets. They are modern in design, all less than five years old, and laid out in pretty avenues with flowering shrubs and shade from tall trees. There are now just ten touring pitches, with 16A electricity and water, and some 200 taken by tour operators. All the shops and amenities are near reception making the accommodation areas quite peaceful and relaxing. There is an amazing variety of activities on offer, and in the main season visitors have the option of using the free bus service to the beach where the site has its own club, Club Emeraude, where you can even go windsurfing at no charge, go kayaking, learn to sail a catamaran or just hire a pedalo. Back on the site, there is a diving club, scuba diving, snorkelling or a boat trip.

You might like to know
There is a PADI and CMAS certified diving centre here. Beginners and more experienced divers are welcome at this excellent centre.

☑ Riding
☑ Pony trekking
☑ Tennis
☑ Cycling (road)
☑ Cycling (mountain biking)
☑ Sports field
☑ Outdoor pool
☑ Crafts
☑ Archery
☑ Sailing

☑ Windsurfing
☑ Diving
☑ Golf
☑ Paintball
☑ Canyoning

Facilities: Two well equipped tolet blocks with facilities for babies and disabled visitors (key access). Laundry. Traditional restaurant and fast food bar, bar and takeaway. Large shop and bazaar (all season). Large aqua park, paddling pools, slides, jacuzzi. Games room. Two play areas. Multisports field. Four tennis courts. Archery. Minigolf. Football. Theatre, evening entertainment, discos, show time spectacular. Riding. Bicycle hire. Watersports. WiFi in bar area. Gas and electric barbecues only.
Off site: Resort of Argelès-sur-Mer with beaches, karting, 10-pin bowling, amusement park and the site's private Eméraude Beach Club, all 2 km. Interesting old town of Collioure close by. Fishing 4 km. Golf 7 km.

Open: 22 April - 29 September.

Directions: Leave A9 motorway at exit 42, take D114, towards Argelès. Leave D114, exit 10 and follow signs for Plage Nord. Site signed after first roundabout and is on right 2 km. after last roundabout. GPS: 42.57093, 3.02906

Charges guide

Per unit incl. 1-3 persons and electricity	€ 26,00 - € 43,00
extra person	€ 6,00 - € 9,00
child (under 5 yrs)	€ 4,00 - € 6,00

FRANCE – Saint Aygulf

Camping Résidence du Campeur

189 les grandes Chateaux de Villepey, RD 7, F-83370 Saint Aygulf (Var)
t: **04 94 81 01 59** e: **accueilcampeur@sandaya.fr**
alanrogers.com/FR83050 **www.sandaya.fr**

Accommodation: ☑Pitch ☑Mobile home/chalet ☐ Hotel/B&B ☐Apartment

This excellent site near the Côte d'Azur will take you away from all the bustle of the Mediterranean coast. Spread out over ten hectares, this is a well equipped holiday destination with pitches arranged along avenues. The bar/restaurant is surrounded by a shady terrace, whilst friendly staff provide an excellent service. A pleasant pool complex is available for those who wish to stay on site instead of going swimming from the Mediterranean beaches. The nearest beach and Saint Aygulf are 2.5 km. away. Activities are organised daily on the site during the summer season. The 177 touring pitches average 100 sq.m. in size and all have electricity connections and, unusually, private sanitary facilities (although washbasins double as dishwashing sinks). There are 235 accommodation units for rent, the majority of which were installed after significant investment by the owners, Sandaya, in 2012.

You might like to know
This region is well known for its fine sandy beaches, and one of the best is just 2.5 km. from this site.

- ☑ Riding
- ☑ Tennis
- ☑ Cycling *(road)*
- ☑ Sports field
- ☑ Outdoor pool
- ☑ Archery
- ☑ Golf
- ☑ Fishing
- ☑ Pétanque
- ☑ Minigolf

Facilities: Private toilet blocks include a washbasin, shower and WC. Laundry area with washing machines. Very well stocked supermarket. Bar/restaurant with evening entertainment. Takeaway (all open all season). Large swimming pool complex with four water slides (high season). Two tennis courts. Minigolf. Boules. Fishing. Bicycle hire. Play area. Games/TV room. WiFi throughout (charged). Only gas or electric barbecues are permitted. Off site: Riding 1.5 km. Golf 2 km. Beach and St Aygulf 2.5 km. Waterskiing nearby.

Open: 31 March - 14 October.

Directions: Leave A8 at Le Muy exit 36 on N555 towards Draguignan then onto the N7 towards Fréjus. Turn right on D7 signed St Aygulf and site is on the right 2.5 km. before the town. GPS: 43.40905, 6.70893

Charges guide

Per unit incl. 2 persons and electricity	€ 25,00 - € 60,00
extra person	€ 3,50 - € 7,00
child (3-7 yrs)	€ 1,00 - € 5,00
dog	€ 5,00

FRANCE – Roquebrune-sur-Argens

Camping les Pêcheurs

F-83520 Roquebrune-sur-Argens (Var)
t: 04 94 45 71 25 e: info@camping-les-pecheurs.com
alanrogers.com/FR83200 www.camping-les-pecheurs.com

Accommodation: ☑Pitch ☑Mobile home/chalet ☐ Hotel/B&B ☐Apartment

Les Pêcheurs will appeal to families who appreciate natural surroundings together with many activities, cultural and sporting. Interspersed with mobile homes, the 110 good sized touring pitches (10A electricity) are separated by trees or flowering bushes. The Provençal style buildings are delightful, especially the bar, restaurant and games room with its terrace down to the river and the site's own canoe station (locked gate). Across the road is a lake with a sandy beach and restaurant. Enlarged spa facilities include a swimming pool, a large jacuzzi, massage, a steam pool and a sauna. Developed over three generations by the Simoncini family, this peaceful, friendly site is set in more than four hectares of mature, well shaded countryside at the foot of the Roquebrune Rock. Activities include climbing the Rock with a guide, trips to Monte Carlo, Ventimigua (Italy) and the Gorges du Verdon, etc. The medieval village of Roquebrune is within walking distance.

You might like to know
There is a diving school on site, so this is a great opportunity to learn.

- ☑ Riding
- ☑ Cycling (road)
- ☑ Sports field
- ☑ Outdoor pool
- ☑ Diving
- ☑ Waterskiing
- ☑ Golf
- ☑ Rafting
- ☑ Canoeing
- ☑ Fishing

Facilities: Modern, refurbished, well designed toilet blocks, baby baths, facilities for disabled visitors. Washing machines. Shop. Bar and restaurant (all open all season). Heated outdoor swimming pool (all season), separate paddling pool (lifeguard in high season), ice cream bar. Games room. Separate adults-only pool and spa facilities. Playing field. Fishing. Minigolf. Activities for children and adults (high season), visits to local wine caves. Only electric barbecues allowed. WiFi throughout (charged). Off site: Bicycle hire 1 km. Riding and golf 5 km. (reduced fees).

Open: 1 April - 30 September.

Directions: From A8 take Le Muy exit, follow N7 towards Fréjus for 13 km. bypassing Le Muy. After crossing A8, turn right at roundabout towards Roquebrune-sur-Argens. Site is on left after 1 km. just before bridge over river. GPS: 43.450783, 6.6335

Charges guide

Per unit incl. 2 persons and electricity	€ 23,00 - € 46,50
extra person	€ 4,00 - € 8,80
child (acc. to age)	free - € 6,75
dog (max. 1)	€ 3,20

alanrogers.com/active

71

FRANCE – Saint Julien-des-Landes

Yelloh! Village Château La Forêt

Route de Martinet, F-85150 Saint Julien-des-Landes (Vendée)
t: 02 51 46 62 11   e: camping@domainelaforet.com
alanrogers.com/FR85820   www.yellohvillage.co.uk/camping/chateau_de_la_foret

Accommodation: ☑Pitch ☑Mobile home/chalet   ☐Hotel/B&B ☐Apartment

Set in the tranquil and beautiful natural parkland surrounding an 19th-century château, this lovely site has 209 large pitches, of which 110 are for touring units. There are also 30 units for rent and 60 pitches are occupied by tour operators. All are on grass and fully serviced including 10A electricity; some are in shady woodland and others, for sun worshippers, are more open. The camping area is only a small part of the 50-hectare estate, with a mix of woodland, open meadows and fishing lakes, all accessible to campers. The many outbuildings around the courtyard have been tastefully converted and include a bar and restaurant in the old stables. There are two swimming pools, one outdoor, the other heated and covered, one on each side of the château. Many sports, activities and entertainment are on offer, which should keep everyone satisfied. Children will have a great time here exploring the vast, unrestricted area and sometimes hidden corners of this site in Swallows and Amazons style. However, parents should note there are open, unfenced fishing lakes and barns with tractors and machinery. The attractive small village with shops and services is within walking distance. The beaches of the Côte de Lumière are just 12 km. away.

You might like to know

Why not visit Le Puy du Fou? The evening spectacle is world class and highly recommended. During the day, the Grand Parc with its wildlife park, its floral park and entertainment is also a trip well worth making.

- ☑ Riding
- ☑ Pony trekking
- ☑ Tennis
- ☑ Cycling (road)
- ☑ Cycling (mountain biking)
- ☑ Sports field
- ☑ Outdoor pool
- ☑ Golf
- ☑ Paintball
- ☑ Aerial walkways
- ☑ Zip wires
- ☑ Canoeing
- ☑ Pedaloes
- ☑ Go-karting
- ☑ Trampolines

Facilities: Three sanitary blocks are newly refurbished and include washbasins in cubicles, with good provision for babies and disabled campers. No motorcaravan service point. Laundry facilities. Shop, bar, small restaurant and takeaway. Two swimming pools (one outdoor, one heated and covered with children's pool and slide). Play area. Regular evening entertainment, children's clubs and disco (July/Aug). Large adventure playground (charged). Trampoline. Games room. Tennis. Boules. Fishing lakes. 6-hole swing golf course (pitch and putt with soft balls) and minigolf. Canoeing trips. Bicycle hire. Free WiFi. Bubble room for hire. Only gas barbecues permitted. Off site: Equestrian centre. Surfschool. Puy du Pou.

Open: 15 May - 15 September.

Directions: Saint Julien-des-Landes is 25 km. west of La Roche-sur-Yon. From La Mothe-Achard take D12 to Saint Julien, turn northeast on D55 at crossroads towards Martinet. Site is on left (signed). GPS: 46.6432, -1.71198

Charges guide

Per unit incl. 2 persons and electricity	€ 18,00 - € 38,00
extra person	€ 5,00 - € 7,00
child (3-7 yrs)	€ 3.10 - € 6,00

FRANCE – Sanchey

Kawan Village Lac de Bouzey

19 rue du Lac, F-88390 Sanchey (Vosges)
t: 03 29 82 49 41   e: lacdebouzey@orange.fr
alanrogers.com/FR88040   www.lacdebouzey.com

Accommodation: ☑Pitch ☑Mobile home/chalet ☐ Hotel/B&B ☐Apartment

Open all year, Camping Lac de Bouzey is 8 km. west of Épinal, at the start of the Vosges Massif. The 147 reasonably level grass pitches are separated by very tall trees and some hedging giving varying amounts of shade. There are 107 for touring, all with electricity (6-10A) and 100 fully serviced. They are on a gently sloping hillside above the lake and there are views over the lake and its sandy beaches. In high season there is entertainment for all ages, especially teenagers, and the site will be very lively. English is spoken. Many watersports may be enjoyed, from pedaloes to canoes, windsurfing and sailing. The large, imposing building at the entrance to the site houses a restaurant and bar with terraces overlooking the lake, and the underground disco. Two bars by the lake would indicate that the lakeside is popular with the public in summer but the camping area is quiet, separated by a road and well back and above the main entrance.

You might like to know

The entertainment team organise nightly shows and a Kids Club. Accompanied walks in the surrounding forest take in the local flora and fauna. Bicycle hire is available and there are many superb drives in the area, including la Route des Crètes.

☑ Riding
☑ Tennis
☑ Cycling (road)
☑ Cycling (mountain biking)
☑ Sports field
☑ Outdoor pool
☑ Archery
☑ Sailing
☑ Paintball
☑ Rock climbing

☑ Hiking
☑ Aerial walkways
☑ Zip wires
☑ Canoeing
☑ Kayaking

Facilities: The refurbished toilet block includes a baby room and one for disabled visitors (there are some gradients). Small, heated section in the main building with toilet, washbasin and shower is used in winter. Laundry facilities. Motorcaravan service point. Shop and bar (all year), restaurant and takeaway (1/3-1/11). Heated pool (1/5-30/9). Fishing. Riding. Games room. Archery. Bicycle hire. Internet access. Soundproofed room for cinema shows and discos (high season). Lake beach, bathing and boating. WiFi.
Off site: Golf 8 km.

Open: All year.

Directions: Site is 8 km. west of Épinal on the D460. From Épinal follow signs for Lac de Bouzey and Sanchey. At western end of Sanchey turn south, site signed.
GPS: 48.16692, 6.35990

Charges guide

Per unit incl. 2 persons and electricity	€ 23,00 - € 34,00
extra person	€ 7,00 - € 10,00
child (4-9 yrs)	free - € 7,00
dog	free - € 4,00

Stowford Farm Meadows

Berry Down, Combe Martin, Ilfracombe EX34 0PW (Devon)
t: **01271 882476** e: **enquiries@stowford.co.uk**
alanrogers.com/UK0690 www.stowford.co.uk

Accommodation: ☑Pitch ☑Mobile home/chalet   ☐Hotel/B&B ☐Apartment

Stowford Farm is a friendly, family park set in 500 acres of the rolling North Devon countryside, available for recreation and walking, yet within easy reach of five local beaches. The touring park and its facilities have been developed in the fields and farm buildings surrounding the attractive old farmhouse and provide a village like centre with a comfortable spacious feel. There are 710 pitches on five slightly sloping meadows separated by Devon hedges of beech and ash. The numbered and marked pitches, some with hardstanding, are accessed by hard roads, most have 10/16A electricity and there are well placed water points. Stowford also provides plenty to keep the whole family occupied without leaving the park, including woodland walks and horse riding from the park's own stables. The Old Stable Bar offers entertainment in high season including barn dances, discos, karaoke and other musical evenings. There is also much for children to do, from the indoor heated pool and under-cover mini zoo (Petorama) where they can handle many sorts of animals (on payment), to the wide range of organised activities on offer.

You might like to know

This site is set in 500 acres of rolling Devon countryside, with mature woodland and lush green (caravan and camping) meadows lined with beech and ash hedges.

- ☑ Riding
- ☑ Pony trekking
- ☑ Cycling *(road)*
- ☑ Sports field
- ☑ Sailing
- ☑ Golf
- ☑ Hiking
- ☑ Fishing
- ☑ Woodland walks

Facilities: Five identical toilet blocks, each looked after by resident wardens, are fully equipped and provide good, functional facilities, each block with laundry facilities. The newest block (in field 5) has under-floor heating and includes facilities for disabled visitors. Extra good facilities for disabled visitors and private family washrooms are beside reception. Shop. Good value takeaway with restaurant area. Bars and entertainment in season. Indoor pool (22x10 m; heated Easter-Oct) at a small charge. Riding. 18-hole pitch and putt. Crazy golf. 'Kiddies kar' track (all charged). Games room. Large play area. WiFi. ATM. Woodland walks. Max. 2 dogs (in separate areas). Off site: Fishing and boat launching 4 miles. Bicycle hire 10 miles.

Open: All year.

Directions: From Barnstaple take A39 towards Lynton. After 1 mile turn left on B3230. Turn right at garage on A3123 and park is 1.5 miles on the right. GPS: 51.174983, -4.05475

Charges guide

Per unit incl. 2 persons and electricity	£ 10,40 - £ 23,00
extra person	free - £ 4,50
child (5-12 yrs)	free - £ 4,50
dog	£ 1,60 - £ 2,60

Woodlands Caravan Park

Holt Road, Upper Sheringham NR26 8TU (Norfolk)
t: **01263 823802** e: **enquiries@woodlandscaravanpark.co.uk**
alanrogers.com/UK3435 www.woodlandscaravanpark.co.uk

Accommodation: ☑Pitch ☑Mobile home/chalet ☐Hotel/B&B ☐Apartment

This pleasant caravan park is set in parkland in the beautiful surroundings of north Norfolk's protected heathland, next to Sheringham Park (National Trust). There are 225 sloping grass pitches with 216 having 10A electricity. They are in two main areas for caravans and motorcaravans (tents are not accepted). A major feature of this site is the superb new toilet block with electronically controlled showers. There are many lovely local walks including one to the beach (1.5 miles). The park is within easy reach of Holt, Cromer and Sheringham, with the major birdwatching areas of Blakeney, Cley and Salthouse also within 30 minutes drive. There is a good bar on site offering entertainment at weekends and the excellent Pinewood Park Leisure Club with 25 m. pool, spa and children's pools and beauty room is adjacent to the park. The Club has swimming pools, sauna, spa, gym and other fitness facilities at a discounted rate for those staying at Woodlands.

You might like to know

The nearby Hilltop Outdoor Centre offers a range of family activities including action-packed Adventure Days.

- ☑ Riding
- ☑ Cycling (road)
- ☑ Crafts
- ☑ Sailing
- ☑ Golf
- ☑ Hiking
- ☑ Fishing
- ☑ Sauna
- ☑ Gym

Facilities: One excellent new toilet block provides all the necessary facilities including those for disabled visitors, baby changing and laundry. Well stocked shop. Gas supplies. Lounge bar and family bar with musical entertainment most weekends. Barbecues. Play area (fenced and gated). Pinewood Park Leisure Club with indoor pool, gym, sauna. etc (all year). Off site: Bicycle hire and fishing 1.5 miles. Norfolk coast, golf and riding 2 miles. Sailing 7 miles. Scenic railway. Stately homes.

Open: 20 March - 31 October.

Directions: From Cromer take the A148 towards Holt, pass signs for Sheringham Park and site is on right (camping sign) just before Bodham village. GPS: 52.92093, 1.17445

Charges guide

Per unit incl. electricity	£ 18,00 - £ 27,00
awning	£ 4,00

Croft Farm Water & Leisure Park

Bredon's Hardwick, Tewkesbury GL20 7EE (Gloucestershire)
t: **01684 772321** e: **enquiries@croftfarmleisure.co.uk**
alanrogers.com/UK4150 www.croftfarmleisure.co.uk

Accommodation: ☑Pitch ☑Mobile home/chalet ☐Hotel/B&B ☐Apartment

Croft Farm is an AALA licensed Watersports Centre with Royal Yachting Association approved tuition available for windsurfing, sailing, kayaking and canoeing. The lakeside campsite has 140 level pitches, of which 80 are for touring units with 10A electricity hook-ups. There are 36 gravel hardstandings with very little shade or shelter.
An upgrade is planned for the fully-equipped gymnasium with qualified instructors, sunbed and sauna. Sports massage, aromatherapy and beauty treatments are available by appointment. The clubhouse has an attractive lakeside terrace and there is a new slipway into the River Avon. Activity holidays for families and groups are organised. Campers can use their own non-powered boats on the lake with reduced launching fees, and there is river fishing. There are plans to include a launch ramp onto the river. Climb Bredon Hill (two miles) for a panoramic view of the Severn and Avon Valleys. Places of interest include Bredon Barn, pottery and church, and the historic town of Tewkesbury with its abbey, theatre and indoor swimming pool.

You might like to know

Accommodation is available in camping pods, with catering from the lakeside café and bar. The watersports school has wide experience in tuition for individuals, families and groups on the lake and nearby River Avon. Sailing boats, windsurfers and canoes

- ☑ Riding
- ☑ Archery
- ☑ Sailing
- ☑ Windsurfing
- ☑ Rafting
- ☑ Canoeing
- ☑ Kayaking
- ☑ Pedaloes
- ☑ Fitness/gym
- ☑ Fishing

Facilities: A recently modernised building has excellent facilities with spacious hot showers. A heated unit in the main building is always open and best for cooler months; this provides further WCs, washbasins and showers, laundry and facilities for disabled visitors. Gas. Watersports centre has shop and conference room. Café/bar (Fri-Sun low season, daily at other times). Takeaway. Gym. Playground. River fishing. Barrier and toilet block key (£5 deposit). WiFi in the clubhouse (free to visitors spending £5 or over). Off site: Pub opposite. Tewkesbury 1.5 miles. Golf 3 miles. Riding 8 miles.

Open: 1 March - 14 November.

Directions: Bredon's Hardwick is midway between Tewkesbury and Bredon on B4080. From M5 exit 9 take A438 (Tewkesbury), at first lights turn right into Shannon Way. Turn right at next lights, into Northway Lane, cross motorway bridge. Turn left into housing estate and cross second bridge. At T-junction turn right on B4080, site is on left opposite Cross Keys Inn. GPS: 52.015967, -2.130267

Charges guide

Per unit incl. 2 persons, electricity and awning	£ 17,00

Tummel Valley Holiday Park

Tummel Bridge, Pitlochry PH16 5SA (Perth and Kinross)
t: **01882 634221**   e: **enquiries@parkdeanholidays.co.uk**
alanrogers.com/UK7305   www.parkdeanholidays.co.uk

Accommodation: ☑Pitch ☑Mobile home/chalet   ☐ Hotel/B&B   ☐Apartment

Set in the Tay Forest Park on the banks of the River Tummel, this large family holiday park is part of the Parkdean Group. Divided into two areas by the roadway, the main emphasis is on chalets to let on the side that overlooks the river. Privately owned caravan holiday homes and touring pitches are on the other, quieter side. The 26 touring pitches, open plan with hardstanding, electricity hook-up and a shared water point, overlook a small fishing lake, which is an added attraction for all the family. On arrival, you should turn right and park, then cross back to book in. The leisure complex with indoor and outdoor activities is on the river side, as is the reception office.

You might like to know

There is a regular bus service close to the site entrance for those wishing to explore the Perthshire Highlands.

- ☑ Riding
- ☑ Cycling *(road)*
- ☑ Sports field
- ☑ Outdoor pool
- ☑ Golf
- ☑ Fishing
- ☑ Nature trails
- ☑ Sauna
- ☑ Adventure play area

Facilities: The very clean toilet block (recently refurbished) has vanity style washbasins, preset showers and a bathroom in each section. Good facilities for disabled visitors. Well equipped laundry. Chemical disposal but no motorcaravan service point. Shop. Riverside entertainment complex with bar and terrace, restaurant and takeaway. Indoor heated pool and toddlers' splash pool. Solarium and sauna. Amusements. Separate area with pool tables. All weather sports court. Adventure play area. Crazy golf. Nature trails. Bicycle hire. Fishing. Note: all venues are non-smoking. Max. 2 dogs per unit. Off site: Golf and riding 10 miles. Buses leave near park entrance.

Open: Late March/Easter - 31 October.

Directions: Travel through Pitlochry. After 2 miles turn left on B8019 to Tummel Bridge (10 miles). Park is on both the left and right. Touring units should turn right and park, then return to reception on the left. GPS: 56.70742, -4.02002

Charges guide

Per unit incl. 4 persons and electricity	£ 13,00 - £ 32,00
dog	£ 2,00 - £ 3,00

Forest Holidays Glenmore

Aviemore PH22 1QU (Highland)
t: **01479 861271** e: **info@forestholidays.co.uk**
alanrogers.com/UK7680 www.forestholidays.co.uk

Accommodation: ☑Pitch ☑Mobile home/chalet ☐ Hotel/B&B ☐Apartment

Forest Holidays is a partnership between the Forestry Commission and The Camping and Caravanning Club. This site is attractively laid out in a fairly informal style in several adjoining areas connected by narrow, part gravel, part tarmac roads, with access to the lochside. One of these, the Pinewood Area, is very popular and has 32 hardstandings (some distance from the toilet block). Of the 220 marked pitches on fairly level, firm grass, 122 have 16A electricity. This site, with something for everyone, would be great for family holidays. The Glenmore Forest Park lies close to the sandy shore of Loch Morlich amidst conifer woods and surrounded on three sides by the impressive Cairngorm mountains. There is regular snowfall in the winter months. The park is conveniently situated for a range of activities, including skiing (extensive lift system), orienteering, hill and mountain walking (way-marked walks), fishing and non-motorised watersports on the Loch.

You might like to know

Why not join in one of the Forest Survival weekends and learn some of the skills you would need to survive alone in the woods? Great fun for all the family!

☑ **Cycling** *(mountain biking)*
☑ **Archery**
☑ **Golf**
☑ **Rock climbing**
☑ **Skiing** *(downhill)*
☑ **Canoeing**
☑ **Fishing**
☑ **Orienteering**
☑ **Den building**
☑ **Abseiling**

Facilities: New toilet and shower blocks. Next to the site is a range of amenities including a well stocked shop (open all year), a café serving a variety of meals and snacks, and a Forestry Commission visitor centre and souvenir shop. Barbecues are not permitted in dry weather. Bicycle hire. Fishing. Sandy beach (Blue Flag). Off site: The Aviemore centre with a wide range of indoor and outdoor recreation activities including skiing 7 miles. Golf within 15 miles. Fishing and boat trips.

Open: All year.

Directions: Immediately south of Aviemore on B9152 (not A9 bypass) take B970 then follow sign for Cairngorm and Loch Morlich. Site entrance is on right past the loch. If travelling in winter, prepare for snow.
GPS: 57.167033, -3.694717

Charges guide

Per unit incl. 2 persons	£ 14,50 - £ 30,00
incl. electricity	£ 19,50 - £ 35,00
extra person	£ 2,75 - £ 4,50
child (5-16 yrs)	£ 2,75 - £ 4,50

Glen Nevis Caravan & Camping Park

Glen Nevis, Fort William PH33 6SX (Highland)
t: **01397 702191** e: **camping@glen-nevis.co.uk**
alanrogers.com/UK7830 www.glen-nevis.co.uk

Accommodation: ☑Pitch ☑Mobile home/chalet ☐Hotel/B&B ☐Apartment

Just outside Fort William, in a most attractive and quiet situation with views of Ben Nevis, this spacious park is used by those on active pursuits as well as sightseeing tourists. It comprises eight quite spacious fields, divided between caravans, motorcaravans and tents (steel pegs required). It is licensed for 250 touring caravans but with no specific tent limits. The large touring pitches, many with hardstanding, are marked with wooden fence dividers, 174 with 13A electricity and 100 also have water and drainage. The park becomes full in the peak months but there are vacancies each day. If reception is closed (possible in low season) you site yourself. There are regular security patrols at night in busy periods. The park's own modern restaurant and bar with good value bar meals is a short stroll from the park, open to all. A well managed park with bustling, but pleasing ambiance, watched over by Ben Nevis. Around 1,000 acres of the Glen Nevis estate are open to campers to see the wildlife and explore this lovely area.

You might like to know
Fort William is the outdoor activity capital of the UK, home to Britain's highest mountain and some of the finest scenery that Europe has to offer.

- ☑ **Cycling** *(mountain biking)*
- ☑ **Diving**
- ☑ **Golf**
- ☑ **Canyoning**
- ☑ **Rock climbing**
- ☑ **Hiking**
- ☑ **Kayaking**
- ☑ **10-pin bowling**
- ☑ **Fishing**
- ☑ **Sailing**
- ☑ **Skiing**
- ☑ **Snowboarding**
- ☑ **Ice Climbing**

Facilities: The four modern toilet blocks with showers (extra showers in two blocks); and units for visitors with disabilities. An excellent block in Nevis Park (one of the eight camping fields) has some washbasins in cubicles, showers, further facilities for disabled visitors, a second large laundry room and dishwashing sinks. Motorcaravan service point. Shop (Easter-mid Oct), barbecue area and snack bar (May-mid Sept). Play area on bark. Off site: Pony trekking, golf and fishing nearby.

Open: 15 March - 31 October.

Directions: Turn off A82 to east at roundabout just north of Fort William following camp sign. GPS: 56.804517, -5.073917

Charges guide

Per person	£ 1,80 - £ 3,00
child (5-15 yrs)	£ 1,00 - £ 1,60
pitch incl. awning	£ 8,30 - £ 11,40
serviced pitch plus	£ 3,50 - £ 4,00

Hoddom Castle Caravan Park

Hoddom, Lockerbie DG11 1AS (Dumfries and Galloway)
t: **01576 300251** e: **hoddomcastle@aol.com**
alanrogers.com/UK6910 www.hoddomcastle.co.uk

Accommodation: ☑Pitch ☑Mobile home/chalet ☐Hotel/B&B ☐Apartment

The park around Hoddom Castle is landscaped, spacious and well laid out on mainly sloping ground with many mature and beautiful trees, originally part of an arboretum. The drive to the site is just under a mile long with a one way system. Many of the 120 numbered pitches have good views of the castle and have gravel hardstanding with grass for awnings. Most have 16A electrical connections. In front of the castle are flat fields used for tents and caravans with a limited number of electricity hook-ups. The oldest part of Hoddom Castle itself is a 16th-century Borders Pele Tower, or fortified Keep. This was extended to form a residence for a Lancashire cotton magnate, became a youth hostel and was then taken over by the army during WW2. Since then parts have been demolished but the original Border Keep still survives, unfortunately in a semi-derelict state. The site's bar and restaurant have been developed in the courtyard area from the coach houses, and the main ladies' toilet block used to be the stables. The park's nine-hole golf course is in an attractive setting alongside the Annan river, where fishing is possible for salmon and trout (tickets available). Coarse fishing is also possible.

You might like to know

Just a two minute walk from the site is an outstanding 9-hole golf course (par 33). The course is landscaped with natural woodland and man-made features, and is surrounded by the River Annan, making it quite a challenging course.

☑ **Riding**
☑ **Pony trekking**
☑ **Cycling** (road)
☑ **Cycling** (mountain biking)
☑ **Golf**
☑ **Hiking**
☑ **Canoeing**
☑ **Fishing**
☑ **Minigolf**
☑ **Large play area**

Facilities: The main toilet block can be heated and is very well appointed. Washbasins in cubicles, 3 en-suite cubicles with WC and basin (one with baby facilities) and an en-suite shower unit for disabled visitors. Two further tiled blocks, kept very clean, provide washbasins and WCs only. Well equipped laundry room at the castle. Motorcaravan service point. Licensed shop at reception (gas available). Bar, restaurant and takeaway (restricted opening outside high season). Games room. Large, grass play area. Crazy golf. Mountain bike trail. Fishing. Golf. Guided walks (high season). Caravan storage. Off site: Tennis nearby.

Open: 1 April - 30 October.

Directions: Leave A74M at exit 19 (Ecclefechan) and follow signs to park. Leave A75 at Annan junction (west end of Annan bypass) and follow signs. GPS: 55.041367, -3.311

Charges guide

Per unit incl. 2 persons	£ 11,50 - £ 18,50
incl. electricity	£ 14,50 - £ 21,50
extra person	£ 3,00
child (7-16 yrs)	£ 1,50

Ballinacourty House Caravan Park

Glen of Aherlow, Tipperary (Co. Tipperary)
t: 062 565 59 e: info@camping.ie
alanrogers.com/IR9370 www.camping.ie

Accommodation: ☑Pitch ☑Mobile home/chalet ☑Hotel/B&B ☐Apartment

Ballinacourty House and its cobble-stoned courtyard form the centrepiece of this south facing park with views of the Galtee Mountains. Accessed by a tree-lined lane, the reception area is in part of the renovated 18th-century building, as is the adjoining restaurant. The park is level with 26 touring pitches with 6A electricity and 19 grassy pitches for tents. Some areas are shaded and there are open spaces to accommodate rallies and larger groups. Self-catering cottages and B&B are also available. This tranquil site is very appealing to families with young children. It is an excellent base from which to tour the Rock of Cashel, the Mitchelstown Caves, Swiss Cottage and the towns of Tipperary, Cahir and Cashel. The management has recently begun to keep farm animals in an enclosed part of the park and intends to enhance the estate's entire old walled garden. Activities in the area include horse riding and trekking, fishing for perch and brown trout, cycling, forest walks, three 18-hole golf courses, leisure centre with swimming pool, cinema, theatre and pottery shop.

You might like to know

There are many superb walking trails in the area, ideal for families, and with plenty of information panels on the flora and fauna of the area, and picnic tables along the way. This corner of Ireland is also a haven for painters and photographers alike.

- ☑ Riding
- ☑ Pony trekking
- ☑ Tennis
- ☑ Cycling (mountain biking)
- ☑ Sports field
- ☑ Outdoor pool
- ☑ Golf
- ☑ Hiking
- ☑ Go-karting
- ☑ Fishing

Facilities: Sanitary facilities provide free hot water and showers. Baby room. Laundry with ironing facilities. Campers' kitchen. Ice pack freezing. Licensed restaurant (early booking advised). Motorcaravan services. Gas supplies. Frisbee golf. TV and games rooms. Picnic benches. Tennis. Play area. Off site: Riding, fishing, golf within 5 miles.

Open: Easter - last Sunday in September.

Directions: Follow the N24 from Tipperary or Cahir to Bansha. Turn on to R663 for 11 km, passing Glen Hotel after 10 km. Follow signs for Ballinacourty House. GPS: 52.41614, -8.21047

Charges guide

Per unit incl. 2 persons and electricity	€ 24,00 - € 27,00
extra person	€ 5,00
child	€ 4,00

Fossa Caravan & Camping Park

Fossa, Killarney (Co. Kerry)
t: **064 663 1497** e: **fossaholidays@eircom.net**
alanrogers.com/IR9590 www.fossacampingkillarney.com

Accommodation: ☑Pitch ☑Mobile home/chalet ☐Hotel/B&B ☐Apartment

This park is in the village of Fossa, ten minutes by car or bus (six per day) from Killarney town centre. Fossa Caravan Park has a distinctive reception building and hostel accommodation, a stimulating play area and shop. The park is divided in two – the touring caravan area lies to the right, tucked behind the main building and to the left is an open grass area mainly for campers. Touring pitches, with 10/15A electricity and drainage, have hardstanding and are angled between shrubs and trees in a garden setting. To the rear at a higher level and discreetly placed are 30 caravan holiday homes, sheltered by the thick foliage of the wooded slopes which climb high behind the park. Not only is Fossa convenient for Killarney (5.5 km), it is also en-route for the famed Ring of Kerry, and makes an ideal base for walkers and golfers. Less than eight kilometres away are the famous walk up the Gap of Dunloe, and Carrantuohill, the highest mountain in Ireland.

You might like to know

The Dingle Peninsula offers fantastic views and winding lanes through small villages down to Slea Head, where you can see the Blasket Islands.

- ☑ **Riding**
- ☑ **Pony trekking**
- ☑ **Tennis**
- ☑ **Cycling** (road)
- ☑ **Cycling** (mountain biking)
- ☑ **Outdoor pool**
- ☑ **Golf**
- ☑ **Hiking**
- ☑ **Fishing**
- ☑ **Mountaineering**

Facilities: Modern toilet facilities include showers on payment. En-suite unit for campers with disabilities. Laundry room. Campers' kitchen. Shop. Takeaway (8/7-25/8). TV lounge. Tennis. Play area. Picnic area. Games room. Security patrol. Off site: Fishing and golf 2 km. Riding 3 km. Bicycle hire 5 km. Woodland walk into Killarney. A visit to Killarney National Park is highly recommended.

Open: 1 April - 30 September.

Directions: Approaching Killarney from all directions, follow signs for N72 Ring of Kerry/Killorglin. At last roundabout join R562/N72. Continue for 5.5 km. and Fossa is the second park to the right.
GPS: 52.07071, -9.58573

Charges guide

Per unit incl. 2 persons and electricity	€ 22,00 - € 26,00
extra person	€ 6,00
child (under 16 yrs)	€ 2,50
hiker/cyclist incl. tent	€ 8,00 - € 9,00

BELGIUM – Jabbeke

Recreatiepark Klein Strand

Varsenareweg 29, B-8490 Jabbeke (West Flanders)
t: 050 811 440   e: info@kleinstrand.be
alanrogers.com/BE0555   www.kleinstrand.be

Accommodation: ☑Pitch ☑Mobile home/chalet ☐ Hotel/B&B ☐Apartment

In a convenient location just off the A10 motorway and close to Bruges, this site is in two distinct areas divided by an access road. The touring section has 137 large pitches on flat grass separated by well trimmed hedges; all have electricity and access to water and drainage. Though surrounded by mobile homes and seasonal caravans, this is a surprisingly relaxing area and the ambience should have been further enhanced in 2011 when a small park was created at its centre. Some children's leisure facilities are provided here, and there is a spacious bar and a snack bar with takeaway. The main site with all the privately-owned mobile homes is closer to the lake, so has most of the amenities. These include the main reception building, restaurants, bar, minimarket, and sports facilities. This is a family holiday site and offers a comprehensive programme of activities and entertainment in July and August. The lake is used for waterskiing and has a supervised swimming area with waterslides (high season) and a beach volleyball area.

You might like to know

There is a sports school where you can learn to water-ski.

- ☑ Riding
- ☑ Tennis
- ☑ Cycling (road)
- ☑ Outdoor pool
- ☑ Waterskiing
- ☑ Golf
- ☑ Paintball
- ☑ Beach volleyball
- ☑ Watersports
- ☑ Teambuilding

Facilities: A single modern, heated, toilet block in the touring area provides the usual facilities including good sized showers (charged) and vanity style open washbasins. Baby room. Basic facilities for disabled campers. Laundry with washing machines and dryer. Dishwashing outside. Additional toilet facilities with washbasins in cubicles are located behind the touring field reception building (open July/Aug). Motorcaravan service point. Bar and snack bar. Play area. Fun pool for small children. In main park: European and Chinese restaurants, bar and snack bar, takeaways (all year). Shop (Easter-end Aug). Tennis courts and sports field. Waterski school; waterski shows (Sundays in July/Aug). Bicycle hire. Cable TV point (included) and WiFi (charged, first hour free) on all pitches. Off site: Riding 5 km. Beach 8 km. Golf and sailing 10 km.

Open: All year.

Directions: Jabbeke is 12 km. southwest of Bruges. From A18/A10 motorways, take exit 6/6B (Jabbeke). At roundabout take first exit signed for site. In 650 m. on left-hand bend, turn left to site in 600 m. GPS: 51.18448, 3.10445

Charges guide

Per unit incl. up to 4 persons

and electricity	€ 20,00 - € 36,00
dog	€ 2,00

Camping Parc La Clusure

Chemin de la Clusure 30, B-6927 Bure-Tellin (Luxembourg)
t: 084 360 050 e: info@parclaclusure.be
alanrogers.com/BE0670 www.parclaclusure.be

Accommodation: ☑Pitch ☑Mobile home/chalet ☐ Hotel/B&B ☐Apartment

A friendly and very well run site, Parc La Clusure is highly recommended. Set in a river valley in the lovely wooded uplands of the Ardennes, known as the l'Homme Valley touring area, the site has 438 large marked, grassy pitches (350 for touring). All have access to electricity, cable TV and water taps and are mostly in avenues off a central, tarmac road. There is some noise from the nearby railway. There is a very pleasant riverside walk; the river is shallow in summer and popular with children (caution in winter). The site's heated swimming pool and children's pool have a pool-side bar and terrace. The famous Grottoes of Han are nearby, also the Euro Space center and Lavaux-Saint Anne castle. Those preferring quieter entertainment might enjoy the Topiary Park at Durbuy.

You might like to know

There is a pleasant riverside walk here – in summer the river is shallow and popular with children.

- ☑ Tennis
- ☑ Cycling (road)
- ☑ Cycling (mountain biking)
- ☑ Outdoor pool
- ☑ Archery
- ☑ Potholing
- ☑ Rock climbing
- ☑ Hiking
- ☑ Canoeing
- ☑ Fishing

Facilities: Three excellent sanitary units, one new and one heated in winter, include some washbasins in cubicles, facilities for babies and family bathrooms. Facilities for disabled campers. Motorcaravan services. Well stocked shop, bar, restaurant, snack bar and takeaway (all 27/4-1/11). Swimming pools (25/4-13/9). Bicycle hire. Tennis. New playgrounds. Organised activity programme including canoeing, archery, abseiling, mountain biking and climbing (summer). Caving. Fishing (licence essential). Free WiFi over site. Barrier card deposit (€ 20). Max. 1 dog in July/Aug. Off site: Riding 7 km. Golf 25 km.

Open: All year.

Directions: Site is signed north at the roundabout off the N803 Rochefort-St Hubert road at Bure, 8 km. southeast of Rochefort with a narrow, fairly steep, winding descent to site. GPS: 50.09647, 5.2857

Charges guide

Per unit incl. 2 persons and electricity	€ 20,00 - € 36,00
extra person (over 2 yrs)	€ 4,00 - € 6,00
dog	€ 4,00 - € 5,00

Camping Floréal La Roche

Route de Houffalize 18, B-6980 La Roche-en-Ardenne (Luxembourg)
t: **084 219 467** e: **camping.laroche@florealclub.be**
alanrogers.com/BE0732 www.florealclub.be

Accommodation: ☑Pitch ☑Mobile home/chalet ☐ Hotel/B&B ☐Apartment

Maintained to very high standards, this site is set in a beautiful wooded valley bordering the Ourthe river. Open all year, the site is located on the outskirts of the attractive small town of La Roche-en-Ardenne, in an area understandably popular with tourists. The site is large with 587 grass pitches (min. 100 sq.m), of which 290 are for touring units. The pitches are on level ground and all have 10/16A electricity and water connections. Amenities on site include a well stocked shop, a bar, a restaurant and takeaway food. In the woods and rivers close by, there are plenty of opportunities for walking, mountain biking, rafting and canoeing. For children there is a large adventure playground which is very popular and during the summer entertainment programmes are organised. The Ardennes region is proud of its cuisine in which game, taken from the forests that cover the area, is prominent; for those who really enjoy eating, a visit to a small restaurant should be planned. English, French, Dutch and German are spoken in reception.

You might like to know

Camping Floréal La Roche is divided into two parts, La Roche I and II. They are located about 500 m. apart, both sites bordering the beautiful River Ourthe.

☑ **Riding**
☑ **Cycling** (road)
☑ **Cycling** (mountain biking)
☑ **Outdoor pool**
☑ **Golf**
☑ **Rafting**
☑ **Potholing**
☑ **Hiking**
☑ **Canoeing**
☑ **Fishing**

Facilities: Six modern, well maintained sanitary blocks provide washbasins (open and in cabins), free preset showers. Facilities for disabled visitors. Baby room. Washing machines and dryers (token from reception). Motorcaravan service point. Well stocked shop (with fresh bread, pastries and newspapers in July/Aug). Bar, restaurant, snack bar and takeaway. At Camping Floréal 2: heated outdoor swimming pool. New wellness facilities with sauna and jacuzzi. Professional entertainment team (during local school holidays). Sports field. Volleyball. Tennis. Minigolf. Pétanque. Dog shower. WiFi. Mobile homes to rent. Off site: Mountain bike and canoe hire 300 m. Golf, riding and bicycle hire 1 km. Indoor pool 2 km. Skiing 15 km.

Open: All year.

Directions: From E25/A26 take exit 50 and follow N89 southwest to La Roche. In La Roche follow signs for Houffalize (beside Ourthe river). Floréal Club Camping 1 is 1.5 km. along this road. Note: go to camping 1 not 2.
GPS: 50.17600, 5.58600

Charges guide

Per unit incl. 2 persons and electricity	€ 14,45 - € 22,85
extra person	€ 3,60
child (3-11 yrs)	€ 2,60

LUXEMBOURG – Wallendorf-Pont

Camping Du Rivage

Echternaccherstroos 7, L-9392 Wallendorf-Pont
t: **836 516** e: **voogt@pt.lu**
alanrogers.com/LU7800 **www.wallendorf-kajaks.de**

Accommodation: ☑Pitch ☐ Mobile home/chalet ☐ Hotel/B&B ☐Apartment

Du Rivage is a small site located on the edge of Wallendorf Pont by a bend in the River Sûre. The owners are friendly and helpful and run a canoe hire business and bicycle hire from the site. The 70 level, grassy touring pitches (all with 6A electricity, long cables needed) are open and undefined. The site is ideal for active families, who will enjoy the kayaking, cycling, fishing. For a small charge, the wellness centre and Internet facilities in the adjacent hotel can be accessed. Motorcaravans over 6 m. long are not accepted as the ground becomes soft in wet weather and the site roads are unsuitable.

You might like to know

Canoeing, mountain biking, hiking and swimming are available on site. Camping guests receive a 10% discount on canoe rentals.

☑ Riding
☑ Tennis
☑ Cycling (road)
☑ Cycling (mountain biking)
☑ Sports field
☑ Outdoor pool
☑ Windsurfing
☑ Waterskiing
☑ Rafting
☑ Potholing

☑ Rock climbing
☑ Hiking
☑ Aerial walkways
☑ Zip wires
☑ Canoeing

Facilities: A modern heated sanitary block with free hot showers, but no facilities for disabled visitors at present. A further small block has cold showers. Bread and milk for sale. Small children's play area. Bicycle hire. Kayak and canoe hire. Bar and takeaway (1/5-30/9). Off site: Hotel next door with Internet and wellness by arrangement. Bus stop by entrance. ATM 2 km.

Open: 14 April - 1 October.

Directions: Take N10 Diekirch to Echternach road. Site is between road and river near centre of Wallendorf Pont and is clearly signed. GPS: 49.8737, 6.29041

Charges guide

Per unit incl. 2 persons and electricity	€ 23,05
extra person	€ 6,25
child (2-12 yrs)	€ 3,50
dog	€ 2,50

NETHERLANDS – Wolphaartsdijk

Camping De Veerhoeve

Veerweg 48, NL-4471 NC Wolphaartsdijk (Zeeland)
t: **0113 581 155**   e: **info@deveerhoeve.nl**
alanrogers.com/NL5580   www.deveerhoeve.nl

Accommodation: ☑Pitch ☑Mobile home/chalet ☐ Hotel/B&B ☐Apartment

This is a family run site near the shores of the Veerse Meer, which is ideal for family holidays. It is situated in a popular area for watersports and is well suited for sailing, windsurfing and fishing enthusiasts, with boat launching 100 m. away. A sandy beach and recreation area, ideal for children, is only a five minute walk. As with most sites in this area there are many mature static and seasonal pitches. However, part of the friendly, relaxed site is reserved for touring units with 90 marked pitches on grassy ground, all with electrical connections. A member of the Holland Tulip Parcs group.

You might like to know
Adults and children alike will love a trip on the historic steam railway, other interesting outings include Miniature Walcheren, the Delta Expo and the fish auction at Colijnsplaat.

☑ **Riding**
☑ **Tennis**
☑ **Cycling** *(road)*
☑ **Sailing**
☑ **Surfing**
☑ **Windsurfing**
☑ **Golf**
☑ **Hiking**
☑ **Canoeing**
☑ **Diving**
☑ **Fishing**

Facilities: Sanitary facilities in three blocks have been well modernised with full tiling. Hot showers are on payment. Laundry facilities. Motorcaravan services. Supermarket (all season). Restaurant and snack bar. TV room. Tennis. Playground and playing field. Games room. Bicycle hire. Fishing. Accommodation for groups. Max. 1 dog. WiFi (charged). Off site: Slipway for launching boats 100 m. Riding 2 km. Golf 5 km.

Open: 1 April - 30 October.

Directions: From N256 Goes-Zierikzee road take Wolphaartsdijk exit. Follow through village and signs to site (one of the site signs is obscured by other road signs and could be missed). GPS: 51.54678, 3.81345

Charges guide

Per unit incl. up to 4 persons and electricity	€ 20,00 - € 27,00
dog	€ 4,00

Camping Lauwersoog

Strandweg 5, NL-9976 VS Lauwersoog (Groningen)
t: **0519 349 133** e: **info@lauwersoog.nl**
alanrogers.com/NL6090 **www.lauwersoog.nl**

Accommodation: ☑Pitch ☑Mobile home/chalet ☐ Hotel/B&B ☐Apartment

The focus at Camping Lauwersoog is very much on the sea and watersports. One can have sailing lessons or hire canoes and, with a new extension, there is direct access to the beach from the site. There are 450 numbered pitches with 225 for tourers. Electricity (10A Europlug) is available at 275 large pitches and 125 have water, drainage, electricity and cable connections. The pitches are on level, grassy fields (some beside the beach), partly separated by hedges and some with shade from trees (cars parked separately). A new building in the marina houses a restaurant, bar, shop and laundry, and also provides beautiful views over the Lauwersmeer. The site's restaurant specialises in seafood and even the entertainment programmes for all ages have a water theme. Youngsters can play on the beach or in a new covered play area, whilst adults may join sailing trips organised from the site, or walk and cycle through the Lauwersmeergebied (a national park) or perhaps, if the tide is low, even walk to Schiemonnikoog.

You might like to know

Enjoy the unique environment of Lauwersmeer National Park and World Heritage Wadden Sea: from seal trips on the Wadden Sea to sailing lessons on the lake. The perfect place for an active yet relaxing holiday.

☑ Riding
☑ Pony trekking
☑ Tennis
☑ Cycling *(road)*
☑ Cycling *(mountain biking)*
☑ Sports field
☑ Outdoor pool
☑ Crafts
☑ Archery
☑ Sailing

☑ Surfing
☑ Windsurfing
☑ Kitesurfing
☑ Diving
☑ Waterskiing

Facilities: The two toilet blocks for tourers provide washbasins, preset showers and child size toilets. Facilities for disabled visitors. Laundry. Campers' kitchen. Ice pack service. Motorcaravan service. Shop. Restaurant (all year), bar and snack bar including takeaway service (1/4-1/10). New play area with bouncy castle. Minigolf at the beach. Sailing school. Canoe hire. Surfing lessons (July/Aug). Horse riding as well as bicycle and go-kart hire on site. Boules. WiFi. Extensive entertainment programme for all ages in high season. Communal barbecue. Torch useful. Off site: Golf 8 km.

Open: All year.

Directions: Follow N361 from Groningen north to Lauwersoog and then follow site signs. GPS: 53.40205, 6.21732

Charges guide

Per unit incl. 2 persons and 10A electricity	€ 29,50
extra person (over 1 year)	€ 4,75
dog	€ 4,75

Molecaten Park Flevostrand

Strandweg 1, NL-8256 RZ Biddinghuizen (Flevoland)
t: **0320 288 480** e: **flevostrand@molecaten.nl**
alanrogers.com/NL6212 **www.molecaten.nl/flevostrand**

Accommodation: ☑Pitch ☑Mobile home/chalet ☐ Hotel/B&B ☐Apartment

Flevostrand is a family site with direct access to Lake Veluwe's sandy beach. All the pitches are situated on spacious grass fields offering ideal opportunities for children to play. You can choose between the area inside the dyke (with 10A electricity) or the beach site (6A electricity) directly at the waterfront. The site has a large marina with a pier and slipway, from where boat launching is possible (boat hire is available). There are various play areas and heated indoor and outdoor pools, and a full bar/restaurant with terrace enjoying beautiful views over the lake. Flevostrand (Flevo beach) is located on land reclaimed from the sea and was developed in the late 1960s. Despite this, trees have matured rapidly in the area, and there are some good walks in the adjacent Wolderwijd forest. Alternatively, and in stark contrast, the Walibi Holland theme park is nearby, and a little further is the old fishing port of Harderwijk, dating back to 1230.

You might like to know

Flevostrand is the place to be for surfers and sailing enthusiasts. If you enjoy watersports, the sailing and surfing courses on offer will help you improve your technique.

- ☑ Tennis
- ☑ Cycling *(road)*
- ☑ Sports field
- ☑ Outdoor pool
- ☑ Archery
- ☑ Sailing
- ☑ Surfing
- ☑ Windsurfing
- ☑ Kitesurfing
- ☑ Waterskiing

- ☑ Golf
- ☑ Paintball
- ☑ Hiking
- ☑ Canoeing
- ☑ Fishing

Facilities: Well maintained toilet blocks provide clean facilities with open style washbasins, preset showers and a baby room. Restaurant with bar and terrace, and takeaway (all 1/4-30/9). Indoor pool and outdoor pool with children's pool (all heated). Games room with air hockey and billiards. Tennis courts. Play areas. Beach volleyball. Bicycle and boat hire. Marina with slipway, surf school and sailing school. WiFi over site (charged). Max. 2 dogs per pitch. Mobile homes and chalets to rent. Off site: Walking and cycling. Walibi Holland theme park. Harderwijk.

Open: 29 March - 1 November.

Directions: From A28 motorway take exit 26 (Harderwijk/Lelystad) and follow signs to Lelystad (N302). After you have crossed the bridge (4.5 km), take the first right turn at the roundabout towards Kampen (Harderdijk). Follow this road to Kampen and turn right after 3 km. Site is well signed. GPS: 52.385401, 5.629088

Charges guideguide

Per unit incl. 2 persons and electricity	€ 17,00 - € 32,00
extra person	€ 3,90
child (2-10 yrs)	€ 2,90
dog	€ 3,90

Recreatiecentrum De Schatberg

Midden Peelweg 5, NL-5975 MZ Sevenum (Limburg)
t: 0774 677 777   e: info@schatberg.nl
alanrogers.com/NL6510   www.schatberg.nl

Accommodation: ☑Pitch ☑Mobile home/chalet ☐ Hotel/B&B ☐Apartment

In a woodland setting of 96 hectares, this friendly, family run campsite is more reminiscent of a holiday village, with a superb range of activities that make it an ideal venue for families. Look out for the deer! A large site with 1,100 pitches and many mobile homes and seasonal or weekend visitors, there are 500 touring pitches. All have electricity (6/10/16A Europlug), cable, water and drainage and average 100-150 sq.m. in size. They are on rough grass terrain, mostly with shade, but not separated. Forty pitches have private sanitary facilities (two with sauna and jacuzzi). Road noise can be heard in parts of this large campsite. The site is well situated for visits to Germany and Belgium, and is easily accessible from the port of Zeebrugge. The surrounding countryside offers the opportunity to enjoy nature, either by cycling or walking. For those who prefer to stay on site, the location is excellent with several lakes for fishing, windsurfing and swimming, plus an extensive range of activities and a heated outdoor swimming pool. A feature at De Schatberg is the attractive restaurant/bar area and the reception and indoor pool (all year), manned by friendly staff.

You might like to know

By the site entrance is a natural pool with a sandy beach, a sunbathing area, a small port and several playgrounds. A little further on is the surfing and fishing lake.

- ☑ Cycling *(road)*
- ☑ Sports field
- ☑ Outdoor pool
- ☑ Windsurfing
- ☑ Golf
- ☑ Aerial walkways
- ☑ 10-pin bowling
- ☑ Fishing
- ☑ Trampoline

Facilities: Five modern, fully equipped toilet blocks, supplemented by three small wooden toilet units to save night-time walks. Family shower rooms, baby baths and en-suite units for disabled visitors. Washing machines and dryers. Motorcaravan service point. Supermarket. Restaurant, bar and takeaway. Pizzeria. Pancake restaurant. Indoor pool. Outdoor pool (1/5-31/8). Trampoline. Play areas. Fishing. Watersports. Bicycle hire. Games room. Bowling. Indoor playground. Entertainment weekends and high season. Water-ski track. WiFi (charged). Off site: Golf 0.5 km.

Open: All year.

Directions: Site is 15 km. west-northwest of Venlo. Leave the A67 Eindhoven-Venlo motorway at Helden, exit 38. Travel north on the 277 for 500 m. and site is signed at new roundabout. GPS: 51.382964, 5.976147

Charges guide

Per unit incl. 2 persons	
and electricity	€ 19,00 - € 31,25
extra person	€ 4,50
dog	€ 5,50

Kennemer Duincamping De Lakens

Zeeweg 60, NL-2051 EC Bloemendaal aan Zee (Noord-Holland)
t: **0235 411 570** e: **delakens@kennemerduincampings.nl**
alanrogers.com/NL6870 www.kennemerduincampings.nl

Accommodation: ☑Pitch ☑Mobile home/chalet ☐Hotel/B&B ☐Apartment

De Lakens is beautifully located in the dunes at Bloemendaal aan Zee. This site has 900 reasonably large, flat pitches of varying sizes, whose layout makes them feel quite private - some come with a ready erected hammock! There are 592 pitches for tourers (542 with 16A electricity) separated by low hedging. This site is a true oasis of peace in a part of the Netherlands usually bustling with activity. From this site it is possible to walk straight through the dunes to the North Sea. Although there is no pool, there is the sea. The reception and management are very friendly and welcoming. A separate area is provided for groups and older teenagers to maintain the quiet atmosphere. The site groups its pitches according to its visitors, for example, there are activity areas, a relaxation area and a family area. Eating facilities are good, with reasonably priced menus, and the supermarket is large and well stocked. A small pizzeria opens several times a week in low season. It is not far to Amsterdam or Alkmaar and its cheese market. We feel you could have an enjoyable holiday here.

You might like to know

Activities are organised for children and there is a playing area just for them on the beach, which features a pirate ship. There is a golf course 10 km. from the site.

- ☑ Cycling *(road)*
- ☑ Crafts
- ☑ Surfing
- ☑ Hiking
- ☑ Swimming
- ☑ Basketball
- ☑ Volleyball
- ☑ Table tennis
- ☑ Kite flying

Facilities: The five new toilet blocks for tourers include controllable showers, washbasins (open style and in cabins), facilities for disabled visitors and a baby room. Launderette. Motorcaravan service points. Bar/restaurant with terrace, pizzeria and snack bar. Supermarket. Adventure playgrounds. Basketball. Bicycle hire. Entertainment programme in high season for all. WiFi over most of site (charged). Range of glamping-style accommodation for rent. Dogs are not accepted. Off site: Beach within 200 m. Fishing 5 km. Golf 10 km.

Open: 28 March - 27 October.

Directions: From Amsterdam go west to Haarlem and follow the N200 from Haarlem towards Bloemendaal aan Zee. Site is on the N200, on the right hand side.
GPS: 52.40563, 4.58652

Charges guide

Per unit incl. 4 persons	€ 25,60 - € 55,00
extra person	€ 5,35

NETHERLANDS – Hilvarenbeek

Vakantiepark Beekse Bergen

Beekse Bergen 1, NL-5081 NJ Hilvarenbeek (Noord-Brabant)
t: 01354 91100 e: info@libema.nl
alanrogers.com/NL5900 www.libema.nl

Accommodation: ☑Pitch ☑Mobile home/chalet ☐ Hotel/B&B ☑ Apartment

Centred around a large lake, Beekse Bergen campsite is part of a large leisure park complex that offers something for all the family, from the Safari Park containing over 1,000 wild animals to Speelland, which caters for children from three to eight years old. The site has 225 touring pitches, all with 4/10A electricity, 100 of which have fresh and waste water connections. They are arranged in small, level, grassy areas surrounded by hedges and mature trees. Several small sandy beaches are to be found around the lake, which can be used for, amongst other things, swimming, windsurfing and fishing. Entry to the safari park and Speelland (playland) are at reduced prices for campers who purchase the extra card when checking in. There are boat trips departing from the Africa club and a road train. The site is well organised, especially with regard to keeping children entertained, and when checking in you receive comprehensive site information in English.

You might like to know

The marina here has 60 berths and can be accessed via the Wilhelmina Canal. At set times each day (10.00, 12.00, 14.00, 16.00 and 18.00), the drawbridge opens so you can sail in and out. A number of berths have power connectors (4A).

- ☑ Riding
- ☑ Pony trekking
- ☑ Cycling *(road)*
- ☑ Sports field
- ☑ Diving
- ☑ Hiking
- ☑ Pedaloes
- ☑ Fishing
- ☑ Basketball

Facilities: Sanitary facilities in the touring area include all the usual facilities including some washbasins in cabins and facilities for disabled visitors. Launderette. Supermarket. Restaurants, cafés and takeaway (weekends only in low seasons). Playgrounds. Indoor pool. Beaches and lake swimming. Watersports including rowing boats and canoe hire. Amusements. Tennis. Minigolf. Fishing. Recreation programme. Bicycle hire. Riding. Bungalows and tents to rent. WiFi (charged). Off site: Golf 5 km. Efteling amusement park.

Open: 21 March - 6 November.

Directions: From A58/E312 Tilburg-Eindhoven motorway, take exit to Hilvarenbeek on the N269 road. Follow signs to Beekse Bergen. GPS: 51.48298, 5.12800

Charges guide

Per unit incl. 2 persons and electricity	€ 15,00 - € 25,00
extra person	€ 7,00
dog	€ 4,00

Camping Wulfener Hals

Wulfener Hals Weg, D-23769 Wulfen auf Fehmarn (Schleswig-Holstein)
t: **043 718 6280** e: **camping@wulfenerhals.de**
alanrogers.com/DE3003 www.wulfenerhals.de

Accommodation: ☑Pitch ☑Mobile home/chalet ☐Hotel/B&B ☐Apartment

This is a top class, all year round site suitable as a stopover or as a base for a longer stay. Attractively situated by the sea, it is a large, mature site (34 hectares) and is well maintained. It has over 800 individual pitches (half for touring) of up to 160 sq.m. in glades. Some are separated by bushes providing shade in the older parts, less so in the newer areas nearer the sea. There are many hardstandings and all pitches have electricity, water and drainage. A separate area has been developed for motorcaravans. It provides 60 extra large pitches, all with electricity, water and drainage, and some with TV aerial points, together with a new toilet block. There is much to do for young and old alike at Wulfener Hals, with a new heated outdoor pool and paddling pool (unsupervised), although the sea is naturally popular as well. The site also has many sporting facilities including its own golf courses and schools for watersports. A member of Leading Campings group.

You might like to know
Swimming lessons for children are available on site.

- ☑ Riding
- ☑ Pony trekking
- ☑ Cycling *(mountain biking)*
- ☑ Outdoor pool
- ☑ Archery
- ☑ Sailing
- ☑ Surfing
- ☑ Windsurfing
- ☑ Kitesurfing
- ☑ Go-karting

- ☑ Diving
- ☑ Waterskiing
- ☑ Golf
- ☑ Canoeing
- ☑ Fitness/gym

Facilities: Five heated sanitary buildings have first class facilities including showers and both open washbasins and private cabins. Family bathrooms for rent. Facilities for children and disabled campers. Beauty, wellness and cosmetic facilities. Laundry. Motorcaravan services. Shop, bar, restaurants and takeaway (April-Oct). Swimming pool (May-Oct). Sauna. Solarium. Jacuzzi. Sailing, catamaran, windsurfing and diving schools. Boat slipway. Golf courses (18 holes, par 72 and 9 holes, par 27). Riding. Fishing. Archery. Well organised and varied entertainment programmes for children of all ages. Bicycle hire. Catamaran hire. Off site: Naturist beach 500 m. Village mini-market 2 km.

Open: All year.

Directions: From Hamburg take A1/E47 north direction Puttgarden, after crossing the bridge to Fehmarn first exit to the right to Avendorf. In Avendorf turn left and follow the signs for Wulfen and the site. GPS: 54.40805, 11.17374

Charges guide

Per unit incl. 2 persons and electricity	€ 14,60 - € 42,11
extra person	€ 4,10 - € 8,60
child (2-18 yrs)	€ 2,30 - € 7,40

GERMANY – Wesel

Erholungszentrum Grav-Insel

Grav-Insel 1, D-46487 Wesel (North Rhine-Westphalia)
t: 028 197 2830 e: info@grav-insel.com
alanrogers.com/DE3202 www.grav-insel.de

Accommodation: ☑Pitch ☑Mobile home/chalet ☐Hotel/B&B ☐Apartment

Grav-Insel claims to be the largest family camping site in Germany, providing entertainment and activities to match, with over 2,000 permanent units. A section for 500 touring units runs beside the water to the left of the entrance and this area has been completely renewed. These pitches, all with 10A electricity, are flat, grassy, mostly without shade and of about 100 sq.m. A walk through the site takes you past a nature reserve and to the Rhine where you can watch the barges. Despite its size, this site is very well maintained, calm, clean and spacious and this is down to the family which started it 40 years ago. This site, on the border with Holland, is an excellent stop over for the north and east of Germany. However, once here, you may decide to stay longer to take advantage of the excellent restaurant (special evenings each week), bird watching on the private reserve or to visit Xanten with its Roman amphitheatre in the archaeological park.

You might like to know

Whether you are looking for relaxation, excitement, education or just some fun, the Duisburg-Nord Landscape Park has all you need.

☑ **Cycling** (road)
☑ **Sports field**
☑ **Outdoor pool**
☑ **Sailing**
☑ **Hiking**
☑ **Fishing**
☑ **Football**
☑ **Children's zoo**
☑ **Beach volleyball**
☑ **Motor boats**

Facilities: Excellent sanitary facilities, all housed in a modern building above which is the bar/restaurant (open all year). Touring area augmented by Portacabin-style units to be renewed. Facilities for disabled visitors. Baby room. Launderette. Motorcaravan service point. Large supermarket. Restaurant/pizzeria. Entertainment area with satellite TV. WiFi. Solarium. Large play area on sand plus wet weather indoor area. Bicycle hire. Boat park. Sailing. Fishing. Swimming. Football (international coaching in high season). Entertainment in high season. Off site: Bus service 500 m. Riding 2 km. The attractive town of Xanten 23 km. Nord Park Duisburg leisure complex 25 km.

Open: All year.

Directions: Site is 5 km. northwest of Wesel. From A3 take exit 6 and B58 towards Wesel, then right towards Rees. Turn left at sign for Flüren, through Flüren and left to site after 1.5 km. If approaching Wesel from west (B58), cross the Rhine, turn left at first traffic lights and follow signs Grav-Insel and Flüren.
GPS: 51.67062, 6.55600

Charges guide

Per unit incl. 2 persons and electricity	€ 15,50
extra person	€ 3,00
child (under 12 yrs)	€ 1,50

GERMANY – Vöhl-Herzhausen

Camping & Ferienpark Teichmann

Zum Träumen 1A, D-34516 Vöhl-Herzhausen (Hessen)
t: **056 352 45** e: **info@camping-teichmann.de**
alanrogers.com/DE3280 www.camping-teichmann.de

Accommodation: ☑Pitch ☑Mobile home/chalet ☐ Hotel/B&B ☐Apartment

Situated near the eastern end of the 27 km. long Edersee and the Kellerwald-Edersee National Park, this attractively set site is surrounded by wooded hills and encircles a six-hectare lake, which has separate areas for swimming, fishing and boating. Of the 500 pitches, 250 are for touring; all have 10A electricity and 50 have fresh and waste water connections. The pitches are on level grass, some having an area of hardstanding, and are separated by hedges and mature trees. At the opposite side of the lake from the entrance, there is a separate area for tents with its own sanitary block. The adjoining national park, a popular leisure attraction, offers a wealth of holiday/sporting activities including walking, cycling (there are two passenger ferries that take cycles), boat trips, cable car and much more. Full details are available at the friendly reception. For winter sports lovers, the ski centre at Winterberg is only 30 km. away from this all-year-round site. With a wide range of facilities for children, this is an ideal family site, as well as being suited to country lovers who can enjoy the endless forest and lakeside walks/cycle tracks in the park.

You might like to know
This site is open all year round and is just 30 km. from the winter sport centre at Winterberg.

☑ **Riding**
☑ **Tennis**
☑ **Cycling** *(road)*
☑ **Golf**
☑ **Hiking**
☑ **Skiing** *(downhill)*
☑ **Canoeing**
☑ **Fishing**
☑ **Cable car**

Facilities: Three good quality sanitary blocks can be heated and have free showers, washbasins (open and in cabins), baby rooms and facilities for wheelchair users. Laundry. Motorcaravan services. Café and shop (both summer only). Restaurant by entrance open all day (closed Feb). Watersports. Boat and bicycle hire. Lake swimming. Fishing. Minigolf. Playground. Sauna. Solarium. Disco (high season). Internet access. Off site: New national park opposite site entrance. Riding 500 m. Golf 25 km. Cable car (bicycles accepted). Aquapark. Boat trips on the Edersee.

Open: All year.

Directions: Site is 45 km. southwest of Kassel. From A44 Oberhausen-Kassel autobahn, take exit 64 for Diemelstadt and head south for Korbach. Site is between Korbach and Frankenberg on the B252 road, 1 km. to the south of Herzhausen at the pedestrian traffic lights. GPS: 51.17550, 8.89067

Charges guide

Per unit incl. 2 persons and electricity	€ 26,00 - € 30,50
extra person	€ 5,90 - € 7,50
child (3-15 yrs)	€ 3,50 - € 4,40
dog	€ 3,60

GERMANY – Neuenburg am Rhein

Gugel's Dreiländer Camping

Oberer Wald 3, D-79395 Neuenburg am Rhein (Baden-Württemberg)
t: **076 317 719** e: **info@camping-gugel.de**
alanrogers.com/DE3455 www.camping-gugel.de

Accommodation: ☑Pitch ☑Mobile home/chalet ☐Hotel/B&B ☐Apartment

Set in natural heath and woodland, Gugel's is an attractive site with 220 touring pitches, either in small clearings in the trees, in open areas or on a hardstanding section used for overnight stays. All have electricity (16A), and some also have water, waste water and satellite TV connections. Opposite is a meadow where late arrivals and early departures may spend the night. There may be some road noise near the entrance. The site may become very busy in high season and on bank holidays but you should always find room. The excellent pool and wellness complex add to the attraction of this all year site. There is a social room with satellite TV where guests are welcomed with a glass of wine and a slide presentation of the attractions of the area. The Rhine is within walking distance. Neuenburg is ideally placed not only for enjoying and exploring the south of the Black Forest, but also for night stops when travelling from Frankfurt to Basel on the A5 autobahn. The permanent caravans, set away from the tourist area with their well-tended gardens, enhance rather than detract from the natural beauty.

You might like to know

Basel, Freiburg, Colmar and Breisach are old towns with minsters and cathedrals. They have a rich cultural heritage, but also boast modern shopping quarters and can be enjoyed in an afternoon.

- ☑ **Riding**
- ☑ **Tennis**
- ☑ **Cycling** (road)
- ☑ **Sports field**
- ☑ **Golf**
- ☑ **Fitness/gym**
- ☑ **Fishing**
- ☑ **Beach volleyball**
- ☑ **Nordic walking**

Facilities: Three good quality, heated sanitary blocks include some washbasins in cabins. Baby room. Facilities for disabled visitors. Laundry facilities. Motorcaravan services. Shop. Excellent restaurant. Takeaway (weekends and daily in high season). Wellness centre. Indoor/outdoor pool. Boules. Tennis. Fishing. Minigolf. Barbecue. Beach bar. Bicycle hire. Community room with TV. Activity programme (high season). Play areas. Off site: Riding 1.5 km. Golf 5 km. Neuenburg, Breisach, Freiburg, Basel and the Black Forest.

Open: All year.

Directions: From autobahn A5 take Neuenburg exit, turn left, then almost immediately left at traffic lights, left at next junction and follow signs for 2 km. to site (called 'Neuenburg' on most signs). GPS: 47.79693, 7.55

Charges guide

Per unit incl. 2 persons and electricity	€ 26,50
extra person	€ 6,50
child (2-15 yrs)	€ 3,00
dog	€ 3,00

GERMANY – Krün-Obb

Alpen-Caravanpark Tennsee

Am Tennsee 1, D-82494 Krün-Obb (Bavaria (S))
t: 088 251 70   e: info@camping-tennsee.de
alanrogers.com/DE3680   www.camping-tennsee.de

Accommodation: ☑Pitch ☑Mobile home/chalet   ☐ Hotel/B&B ☐Apartment

Tennsee is an excellent, friendly site in truly beautiful surroundings high up (1,000 m) in the Karwendel Alps with super mountain views, and close to many famous places of which Innsbruck (44 km) and Oberammergau (26 km) are two. Mountain walks are plentiful, with several lifts close by. It is an attractive site with good facilities including 164 serviced pitches with individual connections for electricity (up to 16A and two connections), gas, TV, radio, telephone, water and waste water. The other 80 pitches all have electricity and some of these are available for overnight guests at a reduced rate. Reception and comfortable restaurants, a bar, cellar youth room and a well stocked shop are all housed in attractive buildings. Many activities and excursions are organised to local attractions by the Zick family, who run the site in a very friendly, helpful and efficient manner.

You might like to know
The mountain station of the nearby cable car affords a wonderful view of the Isar Valley and the Alpine scenery beyond.

- ☑ Riding
- ☑ Tennis
- ☑ Archery
- ☑ Sailing
- ☑ Windsurfing
- ☑ Diving
- ☑ Golf
- ☑ Skiing (downhill)
- ☑ Fishing
- ☑ Paragliding

Facilities: The first class toilet block has underfloor heating, washbasins in cabins and private units with WC, shower, basin and bidet for rent. Unit for disabled guests with the latest facilities. Baby bath, dog bathroom and a heated room for ski equipment (with lockers). Washing machines, free dryers and irons. Gas supplies. Motorcaravan services. Cooking facilities. Shop. Restaurants (waiter, self-service and takeaway). Bar. Youth room. Solarium. Bicycle hire. Playground. WiFi (charged). Organised activities and excursions. Bus service to ski slopes in winter. Off site: Fishing 400 m. Riding and golf 3 km. Discounted entry at Alpspitz-Wellenbad in Garmisch-Partenkirchen and Karwendel Bad in Mittenwald.

Open: All year excl. 6 November - 15 December.

Directions: Site is just off main Garmisch-Partenkirchen-Innsbruck road no. 2 between Klais and Krün, 15 km. from Garmisch watch for small sign Tennsee & Barmsee and turn right there for site. GPS: 47.49066, 11.25396

Charges guide

Per unit incl. 2 persons	€ 23,00 - € 26,00
extra person	€ 7,50 - € 8,00
child (6-16 yrs)	€ 3,00 - € 4,00
electricity per kWh	€ 0,70

Südsee-Camp

Südsee-Camp 1, D-29649 Wietzendorf (Lower Saxony)
t: **051 969 80116** e: **info104@suedseecamp.de**
alanrogers.com/DE3070 www.suedsee-camp.de

Accommodation: ☑Pitch ☑Mobile home/chalet ☐ Hotel/B&B ☐Apartment

Südsee-Camp in the Lüneburger Heide is a large well organised holiday centre where children are especially well catered for. Südsee has its own brochures that include walking, cycling and car tours. There are 497 touring pitches of varying types and sizes, all with electricity and fresh water, drainage and TV connection. Modern sanitary blocks are well maintained and contain all necessary facilities, including some areas specially built for children. Although centred around a large sandy shored lake, complete with shipwreck, the main swimming attraction is the South Sea Tropical swimming pool. This large, well designed, glass roofed complex has pools of different sizes with slides, whirlpools and a pirate ship as well as a sauna, steam bath, sun benches and roof terrace. Adjoining is an outdoor pool. There is a full range of entertainment facilities and programmes for children of all ages. The campsite organises excursions to many interesting locations within the region. Next to the site is a riding school. Reception has a wide range of tourist information brochures and good English is spoken, with the staff only too happy to help and advise. A member of Leading Campings group.

You might like to know

There is a high rope course, with levels for beginners and the more experienced. The highest level is six metres above the ground and has some tricky challenges. It finishes with a 50-metre ropeway back down to the ground.

- ☑ Riding
- ☑ Pony trekking
- ☑ Tennis
- ☑ Cycling *(road)*
- ☑ Sports field
- ☑ Archery
- ☑ Golf
- ☑ Fitness/gym
- ☑ Fishing

Facilities: Twelve modern, well maintained sanitary blocks with all the expected facilities, including those for disabled visitors and private bathrooms to rent. Hot showers need a token. Special areas for children (Kinderland), facilities for babies. Laundry rooms. Kitchens. Choice of bars, restaurants and snack bars. Pool complex (on payment). Soundproofed disco. Fitness room. Bicycle and pedal car hire. Games room. WiFi over part of site (charged). Climbing wall. Jungle golf. Overnight parking outside site.
Off site: Riding adjacent. Fishing 2 km. Golf 12 km.

Open: All year.

Directions: From A7 autobahn take exit 45 towards Bergen and Celle on the B3 (campsite is signed). After 6 km. turn left (site again signed). GPS: 52.931639, 9.965254

Charges guide

Per unit incl. 2 persons and electricity	€ 21,00 - € 49,30
extra person	€ 4,00 - € 5,00
child (2-18 yrs)	€ 2,50 - € 4,00
dog	€ 2,50 - € 3,50

Ferien-Campingplatz Münstertal

Dietzelbachstrasse 6, D-79244 Münstertal (Baden-Württemberg)
t: **076 367 080** e: **info@camping-muenstertal.de**
alanrogers.com/DE3450 www.camping-muenstertal.de/

Accommodation: ☑ Pitch ☐ Mobile home/chalet ☐ Hotel/B&B ☑ Apartment

Münstertal is an impressive site pleasantly situated in a valley on the western edge of the Black Forest. It has been one of the top graded sites in Germany for 20 years, and first time visitors will soon realise why when they see the standard of the facilities here. There are 305 individual pitches in two areas, either side of the entrance road on flat gravel, their size varying from 70-100 sq.m. All have electricity (16A) and 200 have drains, many also with water, TV and radio connections. The large indoor pool with sauna and solarium, and the outdoor pool, are both heated and free. There is a large, grass sunbathing area. The health and fitness centre provides a range of treatments, massages, etc. Children are very well catered for here with a play area and play equipment, tennis courts, minigolf, a games room with table tennis, table football and pool table, and fishing. Riding is popular and the site has its own stables. The latest addition is an ice rink for skating and ice hockey in winter. There are 250 km. of walks, with some guided ones organised, and winter sports with cross-country skiing directly from the site (there are courses in winter for both children and adults, and ski hire).

You might like to know

Whether it involves a mountain bike, Nordic walking poles, a bicycle, your running shoes or hiking boots, a climbing rope or a hang-glider (in summer); skis, snow shoes or crampons (in winter), Münstertal valley is an ideal starting point for an activity holiday.

☑ **Riding**
☑ **Tennis**
☑ **Cycling** (road)
☑ **Outdoor pool**
☑ **Golf**
☑ **Hiking**
☑ **Skiing** (downhill)
☑ **Skiing** (cross-country)
☑ **Fitness/gym**
☑ **Fishing**

Facilities: Three toilet blocks are of truly first class quality, with washbasins all in cabins, showers with full glass dividers, baby bath, a unit for disabled visitors and individual bathrooms, some for hire. Dishwashers in two blocks. Laundry. Drying room. Motorcaravan services. Well stocked shop (all year). Restaurant, particularly good (closed Nov). Heated swimming pools, indoor all year, outdoor (with children's area). New health and fitness centre. Sauna and solarium. Games room. Bicycle hire. Tennis courses in summer. Riding. Ice rink (in winter). WiFi throughout (charged). Off site: Village amenities and train station next to site entrance. Golf 15 km. Freiburg and Basel easy driving distances for day trips.

Open: All year.

Directions: Münstertal is south of Freiburg. From A5 autobahn take exit 64, turn southeast via Bad Krozingen and Staufen and continue 5 km. to the start of Münstertal, where site is signed from the main road on the left. GPS: 47.85973, 7.76375

Charges guide

Per unit incl. 2 persons and services	€ 24,30 - € 30,30
extra person	€ 6,80 - € 8,30
child (2-10 yrs)	€ 4,50 - € 5,20

CZECH REPUBLIC – Vrchlabi

Holiday Park Lisci Farma

Dolni Branna 350, CZ-54362 Vrchlabi (Vychodocesky)
t: 499 421 473   e: info@liscifarma.cz
alanrogers.com/CZ4590   www.liscifarma.cz

Accommodation: ☑Pitch ☑Mobile home/chalet   ☐ Hotel/B&B ☐Apartment

This is truly an excellent site that could be in Western Europe considering its amenities, pitches and welcome. However, Lisci Farma retains a pleasant Czech atmosphere. In the winter months, when local skiing is available, snow chains are essential. The 260 pitches are fairly flat, although the terrain is slightly sloping and some pitches are terraced. There is shade and some pitches have hardstanding. The site is well equipped for the whole family with its adventure playground offering trampolines for children, archery, beach volleyball, Russian bowling and an outdoor bowling court for older youngsters. A beautiful sandy, lakeside beach is 800 m. from the entrance. The more active amongst you can go paragliding or rock climbing, with experienced people to guide you. This site is very suitable for relaxing or exploring the culture of the area. Excursions to Prague are organised and, if all the sporting possibilities are not enough, the children can take part in the activities of the entertainment team, while you are walking or cycling or enjoying live music at the Fox Saloon. The site reports the addition of completely new electrical connections, restaurant, games room and mini-market.

You might like to know
There is an excellent restaurant on site, specialising in traditional Bohemian cuisine.

- ☑ Riding
- ☑ Tennis
- ☑ Cycling (road)
- ☑ Cycling (mountain biking)
- ☑ Archery
- ☑ Sailing
- ☑ Rock climbing
- ☑ Hiking
- ☑ Fishing
- ☑ Paragliding

Facilities: Two good sanitary blocks near the entrance and another modern block next to the hotel, both include toilets, washbasins and spacious, controllable showers (on payment). Child size toilets and baby room. Toilet for disabled visitors. Sauna and massage. Launderette with sinks, hot water and a washing machine. Shop (15/6-15/9). Bar/snack bar with pool table. Games room. Swimming pool (6x12 m). Adventure style playground on grass with climbing wall. Trampolines. Tennis. Minigolf. Archery. Russian bowling. Paragliding. Rock climbing. Bicycle hire. Entertainment programme. Excursions to Prague. Off site: Fishing and beach 800 m. Riding 2 km. Golf 5 km.

Open: All year.

Directions: Follow road no. 14 from Liberec to Vrchlabi. At the roundabout turn towards Prague and site is 1.5 km. on the right.
GPS: 50.61036, 15.60264

Charges guide

Per unit incl. 2 persons and electricity	CZK 294 - 390
extra person	CZK 55 - 65
child (4-15 yrs)	CZK 38 - 45
dog	CZK 45 - 50

CZECH REPUBLIC – Frymburk

Camping Frymburk

Frymburk 184, CZ-38279 Frymburk (Jihocesky)
t: **380 735 284** e: **info@campingfrymburk.cz**
alanrogers.com/CZ4720 www.campingfrymburk.cz

Accommodation: ☑Pitch ☑Mobile home/chalet ☐ Hotel/B&B ☐Apartment

Camping Frymburk is beautifully located on the Lipno lake in southern Bohemia and is
an ideal site. From this site, activities could include walking, cycling, swimming, sailing,
canoeing or rowing and afterwards you could relax in the small, cosy bar/restaurant.
You could enjoy a real Czech meal in one of the restaurants in Frymburk or on site.
The site has 170 level pitches on terraces (all with 6A electricity, some with hardstanding
and four have private sanitary units) and from the lower terraces on the edge of the lake
there are lovely views over the water to the woods on the opposite side. A ferry crosses
the lake from Frymburk where one can walk or cycle in the woods. The Dutch owner,
Mr Wilzing, will welcome the whole family, personally siting your caravan. Children will
be entertained by 'Kidstown' and the site has a small beach.

You might like to know
South Bohemia (Sumava) is the largest
protected natural area in the Czech Republic,
with an impressive mountain range over
120 km. long.

☑ **Cycling** (road)
☑ **Cycling** (mountain biking)
☑ **Crafts**
☑ **Windsurfing**
☑ **Rafting**
☑ **Hiking**
☑ **Canoeing**
☑ **Fishing**
☑ **Volleyball**

Facilities: Three immaculate toilet blocks with
washbasins, preset showers (charged) and an
en-suite bathroom with toilet, basin and shower.
Facilities for disabled visitors. Launderette.
Restaurant and bar (10/5-15/9). Motorcaravan
services. Playground. Canoe, bicycle, pedalos,
rowing boat and surfboard hire. Kidstown.
Volleyball competitions. Rafting. Bus trips to
Prague. Torches useful. Internet access and
WiFi. Off site: Shops and restaurants in the village
900 m. from reception. Golf 7 km. Riding 20 km.

Open: 29 April - 1 October.

Directions: Take exit 114 at Passau in Germany
(near Austrian border) towards Freyung in Czech
Republic. Continue to Philipsreut, from there
follow the no. 4 road towards Vimperk. Turn right
a few kilometres after border towards Volary
on no. 141 road. From Volary follow the no. 163
road to Horni Plana, Cerna and Frymburk. Site is
on 163 road, right after village.
GPS: 48.655947, 14.170239

Charges guide

Per unit incl. 2 persons and electricity	CZK 460 - 810
extra person	CZK 80 - 130
child (under 12 yrs)	CZK 60 - 90

No credit cards.

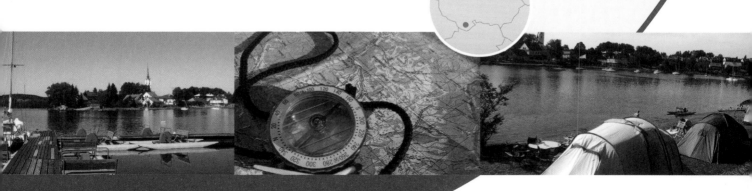

CZECH REPUBLIC – Nové Straseci

Camping Bucek

Tratice 170, CZ-27101 Nové Straseci (Stredocesky)
t: **313 564 212** e: **info@campingbucek.cz**
alanrogers.com/CZ4825 www.campingbucek.cz

Accommodation: ☑Pitch ☑Mobile home/chalet ☐Hotel/B&B ☐Apartment

Camping Bucek is a pleasant, Dutch-owned site 30 km. west of Prague. Its proprietors also own Camping Frymburk (CZ4720). Bucek is located on the edge of woodland and has direct access to a small lake with a private beach. Here you can enjoy canoes and rowing boats which are available to guests free of charge. There are 100 pitches here, many with pleasant views over the lake, and all with electrical connections (6A). Four pitches have their own private sanitary facilities. Shade is quite limited. On-site amenities include an indoor swimming pool, play equipment, trampolines and there is also an activity programme. A short distance from the site is a railway station from which you can catch a fast train into the centre of Prague. The castles of Karlstejn and Krivoklát are also within easy reach, along with Karlovy Vary.

You might like to know
Prague, with its world class museums, galleries and cinemas is just 40 km. away.

- ☑ **Riding**
- ☑ **Cycling** (road)
- ☑ **Cycling** (mountain biking)
- ☑ **Crafts**
- ☑ **Windsurfing**
- ☑ **Hiking**
- ☑ **Canoeing**
- ☑ **Fishing**

Facilities: Renovated toilet blocks with free hot showers. Washing and drying machine. Restaurant and bar. Direct lake access with pedaloes and canoes. Indoor swimming pool with paddling pool. Minigolf. Play area. Trampolines. Activity programme. Walking and cycling opportunities. WiFi throughout. Off site: Revnicov 2 km. with shops (including a supermarket), bars and restaurants. Fishing 3 km. Riding 4 km. Karlovy Vary 10 km. Prague 40 km. Koneprusy caves.

Open: 24 April - 15 September.

Directions: From the west, take no. 6/E48 express road towards Prague. Site is close to this road, 3 km. after the Revnicov exit and is clearly signed from this point. Coming from the east, ignore other camping signs and continue until Bucek is signed (to the north).
GPS: 50.1728, 13.8348

Charges guide

Per unit incl. 2 persons and electricity	CZK 450 - 670
extra person	CZK 75 - 100
child (under 12 yrs)	CZK 50 - 75
dog	CZK 50 - 60

No credit cards.

SLOVAKIA – Liptovsky Trnovec

Mara Camping

SK-03222 Liptovsky Trnovec (Zilina)
t: 044 559 8458 e: info@maracamping.sk
alanrogers.com/SK4915 www.maracamping.sk

Accommodation: ☑Pitch ☑Mobile home/chalet ☐ Hotel/B&B ☐Apartment

This is a bustling Slovakian site beside the Liptovská Mara reservoir, also close to the Tatra Mountains which are popular for climbing, hiking and mountain biking. The lake can be used for sailing, surfing, boating and pedaloes, and some of this equipment may be rented on the site. Bicycles are also available for hire. There are 250 pitches, all used for touring units and with 14A electricity. With tarmac access roads, the level pitches are on a circular, grassy field and as pitching is rather haphazard, the site can become crowded in high season. Mature trees provide some shade, but in general this is an open site. English is spoken. This is a busy holiday site, but strict rules apply about evening rest, so it is also suitable for families with younger children. There are several bars with snack and takeaway services on site with a restaurant nearby (300 m). The site is close to the historic cities of Liptovsky Mikulás (6 km), Vlkolinec (on the UNESCO World Heritage list) and Pribylina.

You might like to know
This site is situated on the banks of the Liptovsky Mara dam, the largest in Slovakia. The reservoir is popular with lovers of water and outdoor sports. Liptovsky Mara enjoys ideal conditions for yachting and windsurfing, with opportunities for fishing, sightseeing trips and mountain biking.

- ☑ **Cycling** *(mountain biking)*
- ☑ **Sailing**
- ☑ **Windsurfing**
- ☑ **Golf**
- ☑ **Rafting**
- ☑ **Rock climbing**
- ☑ **Hiking**
- ☑ **Canoeing**
- ☑ **Kayaking**
- ☑ **Fishing**

Facilities: Two good modern toilet blocks have British style toilets, washbasins in cabins and showers. Facilities for disabled visitors. Laundry and kitchen. Motorcaravan service. Bar with covered terrace and takeaway service. Good adventure playground. Minigolf. Fishing. Bicycle hire. Canoe hire, jetski and boat rental. Games room with arcade machines. Beach. WiFi. Off site: Restaurant 300 m. New Tatralandia Aqua Park nearby. Walking in the Lower Tatra Mountains, or serious climbing in the Higher Tatra Mountains.

Open: 30 April - 30 October.

Directions: From E50 road take exit for Liptovsky Mikulás and turn left towards Liptovsky Trnovec on 584 road. Continue alongside the lake to site on the left.
GPS: 49.111135, 19.545946

Charges guide

Per unit incl. 2 persons and electricity	€ 20,00
extra person	€ 10,00
child (3-15 yrs)	€ 3,50
dog	€ 2,00

Fårup Sø Camping

Fårupvej 58, DK-7300 Jelling (Vejle)
t: 75 87 13 44 e: faarup-soe@dk-camp.dk
alanrogers.com/DK2048 www.faarup-soe.dk-camp.dk

Accommodation: ☑Pitch ☑Mobile home/chalet ☐Hotel/B&B ☐Apartment

Fårup Sø Camping is a friendly and welcoming, family run site next to the beautiful Fårup Lake and is in a good location for visiting some of Denmark's best known attractions such as Legoland and the Lion Park. There are 250 grassy pitches, mostly on terraces (from top to bottom the height difference is 53 m). Some have beautiful views of the Fårup Lake. There are 200 pitches for touring units, all with 16A electricity, and some tent pitches without electricity. A heated swimming pool (min. 25°C), a whirlpool (free of charge) and an indoor play area for children are popular, as are the available activities, many associated with the lake. Next to the top toilet block is a barbecue area with a terrace and good views. A neighbour rents out water bikes and takes high season excursions onto the lake with a real Viking Ship which campers can join. During the last weekend of May the site celebrates the Jelling Musical Festival when it is advisable to book in advance. This family site is ideal for those who want to enjoy a relaxed holiday on the lakeside beaches or go walking or cycling through the surrounding countryside. Fishing is a very popular activity and rods and bait are available at the shop.

You might like to know
There is an excellent animal park just 8 km. from this site.

- ☑ Riding
- ☑ Pony trekking
- ☑ Cycling (road)
- ☑ Sports field
- ☑ Outdoor pool
- ☑ Golf
- ☑ Canoeing
- ☑ Pedaloes
- ☑ Fishing
- ☑ Boat launching

Facilities: One modern and one older toilet block have British style toilets, open style washbasins and controllable hot showers. Family shower rooms. Baby room. Facilities for disabled visitors. Laundry. Campers' kitchen. Motorcaravan services. Shop (bread to order). Heated swimming pool and whirlpool. Indoor play area. Playgrounds. Games room. Lake with fishing, watersports and Viking ship. Three play areas. Activities for children (high season). WiFi (charged). Off site: Golf and riding 2 km. Lion Park 8 km. Boat launching 10 km. Legoland 20 km.

Open: 1 April - 9 September.

Directions: From Vejle take the 28 road towards Billund. In Skibet turn right towards Fårup Sø, Jennum and Jelling and follow the signs to Fårup Sø. GPS: 55.73614, 9.41777

Charges guide

Per unit incl. 2 persons and electricity	DKK 181 - 226
extra person	DKK 73
child (1-11 yrs)	DKK 43
dog	DKK 15

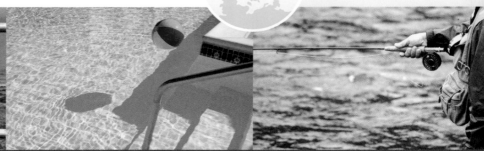

DENMARK – Nykobing Mors

Jesperhus Feriecenter & Camping

Legindvej 30, DK-7900 Nykobing Mors (Viborg)
t: **96 70 14 00** e: **jesperhus@jesperhus.dk**
alanrogers.com/DK2140 www.jesperhus.dk

Accommodation: ☑Pitch ☑Mobile home/chalet ☐Hotel/B&B ☐Apartment

Jesperhus is an extensive, well organised and busy site with many leisure activities, adjacent to Blomsterpark (Northern Europe's largest flower park). This TopCamp site has 662 numbered pitches, mostly in rows with some terracing, divided by shrubs and trees and with shade in parts. Many pitches are taken by seasonal, tour operator or rental units, so advance booking is advised for peak periods. Electricity (6A) is available on all pitches and water points are in all areas. There are 300 pitches available with full services. With all the activities at this site, an entire holiday could be spent here regardless of the weather, although Jesperhus is also an excellent centre for touring. The indoor and outdoor pool complex has three pools, diving boards, water slides with the 'black hole', spa pools, saunas and a solarium. Although it may appear to be just part of Jutland, Mors is an island in its own right surrounded by the lovely Limfjord. It is joined to the mainland by a fine 2,000 m. bridge at the end of which are signs to Blomsterpark (which also houses a bird zoo, Butterfly World, terrarium and aquarium) and the campsite – both under the same ownership.

You might like to know
The indoor facilities provide a wide range of sporting activities including squash and climbing.

- ☑ Riding
- ☑ Tennis
- ☑ Cycling (road)
- ☑ Cycling (mountain biking)
- ☑ Outdoor pool
- ☑ Golf
- ☑ Go-karting
- ☑ 10-pin bowling
- ☑ Fishing
- ☑ Beach volleyball

Facilities: Four good sanitary units are cleaned three times daily. Facilities include washbasins in cubicles or with divider/curtain, family and whirlpool bathrooms (on payment), suites for babies and disabled visitors. Free sauna. Superb kitchens and a fully equipped laundry. Supermarket (1/4-1/11). Restaurant. Bar. Café, takeaway. Pool complex with spa facilities. Bowling. Minigolf. Tennis. Go-karts and other outdoor sports. Children's 'playworld'. Playgrounds. Pets corner. Golf. Fishing pond. Practice golf (3 holes). Off site: Beach and riding 2 km. Bicycle hire 6 km.

Open: All year.

Directions: From south or north, take road 26 to Salling Sund bridge, site is signed Jesperhus, just north of the bridge. GPS: 56.75082, 8.81580

Charges guide

Per person	DKK 75
child (1-11 yrs)	DKK 55
pitch	free - DKK 50
electricity	DKK 40

Klim Strand Camping

Havvejen 167, Klim Strand, DK-9690 Fjerritslev (Nordjylland)
t: 98 22 53 40   e: ksc@klim-strand.dk
alanrogers.com/DK2170 www.klim-strand.dk

Accommodation: ☑Pitch ☑Mobile home/chalet   ☐ Hotel/B&B ☐Apartment

A large family holiday site right beside the sea, Klim Strand is a paradise for children.
It is a privately owned TopCamp site with a full complement of quality facilities, including
its own fire engine and trained staff. The site has 460 numbered touring pitches, all with
electricity (10A), laid out in rows, many divided by trees and hedges, with shade in parts.
Some 220 of these are extra large (180 sq.m) and fully serviced with electricity, water,
drainage and TV hook-up. On-site activities include an outdoor water slide complex,
an indoor pool, tennis courts and pony riding (all free). A wellness spa centre including
a pirate-themed indoor play hall is a recent addition. For children there are numerous
play areas, an adventure playground with aerial cable ride and a roller skating area.
There is a kayak school and a large bouncy castle for toddlers. Live music and dancing
are organised twice a week in high season. Suggested excursions include trips to
offshore islands, visits to local potteries, a brewery museum and birdwatching on
the Bygholm Vejle. A member of Leading Campings group.

You might like to know
The North Sea Oceanarium is the biggest
aquarium in northern Europe.

- ☑ **Riding**
- ☑ **Tennis**
- ☑ **Cycling** *(road)*
- ☑ **Outdoor pool**
- ☑ **Golf**
- ☑ **Kayaking**
- ☑ **Fitness/gym**
- ☑ **Fishing**

Facilities: Two good, large, heated toilet blocks
are central, with spacious showers and some
washbasins in cubicles. Separate children's
room. Baby rooms. Bathrooms for families (some
charged) and disabled visitors. Laundry. Well
equipped kitchens and barbecue areas. TV
lounges. Motorcaravan services. Pizzeria.
Supermarket, restaurant and bar (all season).
Pool complex. Wellness centre with sauna,
solariums, whirlpool bath, fitness room and
indoor play hall. TV rental. Play areas. Crèche.
Bicycle hire. Cabins to rent. WiFi (charged).
Off site: Golf 10 km. Boat launching 25 km.

Open: 30 March - 21 October.

Directions: Turn off Thisted-Fjerritslev 11 road to
Klim from where site is signed.
GPS: 57.133333, 9.166667

Charges guide

Per unit incl. 2 persons and electricity	€ 31,00 - € 50,30
extra person	€ 11,00
child (1-11 yrs)	€ 8,20

Fornæs Camping

Stensmarkvej 36, DK-8500 Grenå (Århus)
t: **86 33 23 30**   e: **fornaes@1031.inord.dk**
alanrogers.com/DK2070   www.fornaesfamiliecamping.dk

Accommodation: ☑Pitch ☑Mobile home/chalet   ☐Hotel/B&B   ☐Apartment

In the grounds of a former farm, Fornæs Camping is about 5 km. from Grenå. From reception, a wide gravel access road descends through a large grassy field to the sea. Pitches to the left are mostly level, to the right slightly sloping with some terracing and views of the Kattegat. The rows of pitches are divided into separate areas by colourful bushes and each row is marked by a concrete tub containing a young tree and colourful flowers. Fornæs has 320 pitches of which 240 are for tourers, the others being used for seasonal visitors. All touring pitches have 10A electricity. At the foot of the site is a pebble beach with a large grass area behind it for play and sunbathing. There is also an attractive outdoor pool near the entrance with two slides, a paddling pool, sauna, solarium and whirlpool. Here a comprehensive room serves as a restaurant, takeaway and bar, and in a former barn there is a new games room. Fornæs provides a good base from which to explore this part of Denmark or for taking the ferry to Hjelm island or to Sweden.

You might like to know
There are a number of attractive, fully equipped wooden chalets on this site, all available for rent.

- ☑ Riding
- ☑ Outdoor pool
- ☑ Sailing
- ☑ Golf
- ☑ Fishing
- ☑ Minigolf
- ☑ Sauna
- ☑ Adventure playground

Facilities: Two partly refurbished toilet blocks have British style toilets, washbasins in cabins and controllable hot showers. Children's section and baby room. Family shower rooms. Facilities for disabled visitors. Fully equipped laundry. Campers' kitchen. Motorcaravan service point. Shop. Café/grill with bar and takeaway (evenings). Swimming pool (80 sq.m) with paddling pool. Sauna and solarium. Play area and adventure playground. Games room with satellite TV. Minigolf. Fishing. Watersports. Off site: Golf and riding 5 km.

Open: 15 March - 20 September.

Directions: From Århus follow the 15 road towards Grenå and then the 16 road towards town centre. Turn north and follow signs for Fornæs and the site. GPS: 56.45602, 10.94107

Charges guide

Per person	DKK 67 - 75
child (1-12 yrs)	DKK 38 - 42
electricity (10A)	DKK 28

Credit cards 5% surcharge.

Odda Camping

Borsto, N-5750 Odda (Hordaland)
t: 41 32 16 10 e: post@oppleve.no
alanrogers.com/NO2320 www.oppleve.no

Accommodation: ☑Pitch ☑Mobile home/chalet ☐Hotel/B&B ☐Apartment

Bordered by the Folgefonna glacier to the west and the Hardangervidda plateau to the east and south, Odda is an industrial town with electro-chemical enterprises based on zinc mining and hydro-electric power. This site has been attractively developed on the town's southern outskirts. It is spread over 2.5 acres of flat, mature woodland, which is divided into small clearings by massive boulders. Access is by well tended tarmac roads which wind their way among the trees and boulders. There are 55 tourist pitches including 36 with electricity. The site fills up in the evenings and can be crowded with facilities stretched from the end of June to early August. The site is just over a kilometre from the town centre, on the shores of the Sandvin lake (good salmon and trout fishing) and on the minor road leading up the Buar Valley to the Buar glacier, Vidfoss Falls and Folgefonna ice cap. It is possible to walk to the ice face but in the later stages this is quite hard going! At the turn of the century, Odda was one of the most popular destinations for the European upper classes – the magnificent and dramatic scenery is still there, together with the added interest of the industrial impact which is well recorded at the industrial museum at Tyssedal.

Facilities: A single timber building at the entrance houses the reception office and the simple, but clean, sanitary facilities which provide for each sex, two WCs, one hot shower (on payment) and three open washbasins. A new building provides additional unisex toilets, showers and laundry facilities. Small kitchen. Mini shop. Off site: Town facilities close.

Open: All year.

Directions: Site is on the southern outskirts of Odda, signed off road to Buar, with a well marked access. GPS: 60.05320, 6.54380

Charges guide

Per person	NOK 10
tent and car	NOK 110
caravan or motorcaravan	NOK 130
electricity	NOK 40

No credit cards.

You might like to know

The campsite is open all year, offering a wide range of summer and winter activities and the chance to experience nature and the great outdoors. These include winter orienteering and tours to waterfalls and glaciers.

- ☑ Riding
- ☑ Tennis
- ☑ Cycling (mountain biking)
- ☑ Archery
- ☑ Paintball
- ☑ Rafting
- ☑ Rock climbing
- ☑ Hiking
- ☑ Skiing (downhill)
- ☑ Snowboarding

- ☑ Canoeing
- ☑ Water rugby
- ☑ Glacier walks
- ☑ Fishing
- ☑ Swimming

NORWAY – Lærdal

Lærdal Ferie & Fritidspark

Grandavegens, N-6886 Lærdal (Sogn og Fjordane)
t: 57 66 66 95 e: info@laerdalferiepark.com
alanrogers.com/NO2375 www.laerdalferiepark.com

Accommodation: ☑Pitch ☑Mobile home/chalet ☑Hotel/B&B ☑Apartment

This site is beside the famous Sognefjord, the longest fjord in the world. It is ideally situated if you want to explore the glaciers, fjords and waterfalls of the region. The 100 pitches are level with well trimmed grass, connected by tarmac roads and are suitable for tents, caravans and motorcaravans. There are 80 electrical hook-ups. The fully licensed restaurant serves traditional meals as well as snacks and pizzas. The pretty little village of Laerdal, only 400 m. away, is well worth a visit. A walk among the old, small wooden houses is a pleasant and interesting experience. You can hire boats on the site for short trips on the fjord. Guided hiking, cycling and fishing trips are also available. The site also provides cabins, flats and rooms to rent, plus a brand new motel, all very modern and extremely tastefully designed.

You might like to know

Lærdal Ferie & Fritidspark is situated right on the famous Sognefjord, the longest and the deepest fjord in the world. The Norwegian Wild Salmon Centre is just 400 m. away.

- ☑ Riding
- ☑ Tennis
- ☑ Cycling (road)
- ☑ Cycling (mountain biking)
- ☑ Golf
- ☑ Hiking
- ☑ Canoeing
- ☑ Fishing
- ☑ Beach volleyball

Facilities: Two modern and well decorated sanitary blocks with washbasins (some in cubicles), showers on payment, and toilets. Facilities for disabled visitors. Children's room. Washing machine and dryer. Kitchen. Motorcaravan services. Small shop. Bar, restaurant and takeaway (20/5-5/9). TV room. Playground. Motorboats, rowing boats, canoes, bicycles and pedal cars for hire. Bicycle hire. Fishing. WiFi at reception. Off site: Cruises on the Sognefjord 400 m. The Norwegian Wild Salmon Centre 400 m. Riding 500 m. Golf 12 km. The Flåm railway 40 km.

Open: All year, by telephone request 1/11-14/3.

Directions: Site is on road 5 (from the Oslo-Bergen road, E16) 400 m. north of Laerdal village centre. GPS: 61.10037, 7.46986

Charges guide

Per unit incl. 2 persons and electricity	NOK 210
extra person	NOK 50
child (4-15 yrs)	NOK 25

Kjørnes Camping

N-6856 Sogndal (Sogn og Fjordane)
t: 57 67 45 80 e: camping@kjornes.no
alanrogers.com/NO2390 www.kjornes.no

Accommodation: ☑Pitch ☑Mobile home/chalet ☐ Hotel/B&B ☑Apartment

Kjørnes Camping is idyllically situated on the Sognefjord, 3 km. from the centre of Sogndal. It occupies a long open meadow which is terraced down to the waterside. The site has 100 pitches for camping units (all with electricity), 14 cabins and two apartments for rent. Located at the very centre of the 'fjord kingdom' by the main no. 5 road, this site is the ideal base from which to explore the Sognefjord. You are within a short drive (maximum one hour) from all the major attractions including the Jostedal glacier, the Nærøyfjord, the Flåm Railway, the Urnes Stave Church and Sognefjellet. This site is ideal for those who enjoy peace and quiet, lovely scenery or a spot of fishing. Access is via a narrow lane with passing places, which drops down towards the fjord three kilometres from Sogndal.

You might like to know

The Sogn Folkemuseum is a fascinating museum with activities for all ages. Its exhibits include old homes, buildings and farm animals, and it explains how the local farmers worked the land in the 1800s.

- ☑ Cycling *(road)*
- ☑ Cycling *(mountain biking)*
- ☑ Rafting
- ☑ Rock climbing
- ☑ Hiking
- ☑ Aerial walkways
- ☑ Fishing
- ☑ Glacier walks
- ☑ Swimming
- ☑ Local sports hall

Facilities: A high quality sanitary building was added in 2008. Baby room. Facilities for disabled visitors. A new building provides a kitchen with cooking facilities, dishwasher, a dining area overlooking the fjord, and laundry facilities. Small shop (20/6-20/8). Satellite TV, WiFi throughout (free). Off site: Hiking, glacier walks, climbing, rafting, walking around Sognefjord. Details from reception. Bicycle hire 3 km.

Open: 1 May - 1 October.

Directions: Site is off the Rv 5, 3 km. east of Sogndal, 8 km. west of Kaupanger.
GPS: 61.21164, 7.12108

Charges guide

Per unit incl. 2 persons and electricity	NOK 270
extra person	NOK 15
child (4-16 yrs)	NOK 10

Trollveggen Camping

Horgheimseidet, N-6300 Åndalsnes (Møre og Romsdal)
t: **71 22 37 00** e: **post@trollveggen.no**
alanrogers.com/NO2452 www.trollveggen.no

Accommodation: ☑Pitch ☑Mobile home/chalet ☐ Hotel/B&B ☑ Apartment

The location of this site provides a unique experience – it is set at the foot of the famous vertical cliff of Trollveggen (the Troll Wall), which is Europe's highest vertical mountain face. The site is pleasantly laid out in terraces with level grass pitches. The facility block, four cabins and reception are all very attractively built with grass roofs. Beside the river is an attractive barbecue area where barbecue parties are sometimes arranged. This site is a must for people who love nature. The site is surrounded by the Troll Peaks and the Romsdalshorn Mountains with the rapid river of Rauma flowing by. Here in the beautiful valley of Romsdalen you have the ideal starting point for trips to many outstanding attractions such as 'The Troll Road' to Geiranger or to the Mardalsfossen waterfalls. In the mountains there are nature trails of various lengths and difficulties. The campsite owners are happy to help you with information. The town of Åndalsnes is 10 km. away and has a long tourism tradition as a place to visit. It is situated in the inner part of the beautiful Romsdalfjord and has a range of shops and restaurants.

You might like to know

Trollveggen Camping offers a wide range of activities in the area, together with Romsdal Aktiv (www.romsdalaktiv.com) and Ski Romsdal (www.skiromsdal.no).

☑ **Cycling** (mountain biking)
☑ **Golf**
☑ **Rafting**
☑ **Rock climbing**
☑ **Hiking**
☑ **Skiing** (downhill)
☑ **Skiing** (cross-country)
☑ **Snowboarding**
☑ **Canoeing**
☑ **Kayaking**

☑ **Fishing**
☑ **Glacier walking**
☑ **Paragliding**
☑ **Base jumping**

Facilities: One heated toilet block provides washbasins, some in cubicles, and showers on payment. Family room with baby bath and changing mat, plus facilities for disabled visitors. Communal kitchen with cooking rings, small ovens, fridge and sinks (free hot water). Laundry facilities. Motorcaravan service point. Barbecue area (covered). Playground. Duck pond. WiFi throughout (free). Off site: Climbing, glacier walking and hiking. Fjord fishing. Sightseeing trips. The Troll Road. Mardalsfossen (waterfall). Geiranger and Åndalsnes.

Open: 10 May - 20 September.

Directions: Site is located on the E136 road, 10 km. south of Åndalsnes. It is signed. GPS: 62.49444, 7.758333

Charges guide

Per unit incl. 2 persons and electricity	NOK 229
extra person (over 4 yrs)	NOK 12

Neset Camping

N-4741 Byglandsfjord (Aust-Agder)
t: **37 93 42 55** e: **post@neset.no**
alanrogers.com/NO2610 www.neset.no

Accommodation: ☑Pitch ☑Mobile home/chalet ☐Hotel/B&B ☐Apartment

On a semi-promontory on the shores of the 40 km. long Byglandsfjord, Neset is a good centre for activities or as a stop en route north from the ferry port of Kristiansand (from England or Denmark). Neset is situated on well kept grassy meadows by the lake shore, with water on three sides and the road on the fourth, and provides 200 unmarked pitches with electricity and cable TV available. The main building houses reception, a small shop and a restaurant with fine views over the water. This is a well run, friendly site where one could spend an active few days. Byglandsfjord offers good fishing (mainly trout) and the area has marked trails for cycling, riding or walking in an area famous for its minerals.

You might like to know
The Setesdal valley is home to a number of museums devoted to minerals, silversmithing and other forms of art and handicraft.

☑ Riding
☑ Cycling *(road)*
☑ Cycling *(mountain biking)*
☑ Sailing
☑ Rafting
☑ Rock climbing
☑ Hiking
☑ Skiing *(cross-country)*
☑ Canoeing
☑ Fishing

Facilities: Three modern sanitary blocks which can be heated, all with comfortable hot showers (some on payment), washing up facilities (metered hot water) and a kitchen. Restaurant and takeaway (15/6-15/8). Shop (1/5-1/10). Campers' kitchen. Playground. Lake swimming, boating and fishing. Excellent new barbecue area and hot tub. Bicycle, canoe and pedalo hire. Climbing, rafting and canoeing courses arranged (including trips to see beavers and elk). Cross-country skiing possible in winter. Off site: Rock climbing wall. Marked forest trails.

Open: All year.

Directions: Site is on route 9, 2.5 km. north of the town of Byglandsfjord on the eastern shores of the lake. GPS: 58.68848, 7.80132

Charges guide

Per unit incl. 2 persons
and electricity   NOK 30

Röstånga Camping & Bad

Blinkarpsvägen 3, S-268 68 Röstånga (Skåne Län)
t: 043 591 064 e: nystrand@msn.com
alanrogers.com/SW2630 www.rostangacamping.se

Accommodation: ☑Pitch ☑Mobile home/chalet ☐ Hotel/B&B ☐Apartment

Beside the Söderåsen National Park, this scenic campsite has its own fishing lake and many activities for the whole family. There are 180 large, level, grassy pitches with electricity (10A) and a quiet area for tents with a view over the fishing lake. The tent area has its own service building and several barbecue places. A large holiday home and 21 pleasant cabins are available to rent all year round. A pool complex adjacent to the site provides a 50 m. swimming pool, three children's pools and a water slide, all heated during peak season. Activities are arranged on the site in high season, including a children's club with exciting activities such as treasure hunts and gold panning, and for adults, aquarobics, Nordic walking and tennis. The Söderåsen National Park offers hiking and bicycle trails. The friendly staff will be happy to help you to plan interesting excursions in the area.

You might like to know

An activity leader organises a wide selection of activities and events, which are free of charge for all campers.

- ☑ Riding
- ☑ Pony trekking
- ☑ Tennis
- ☑ Cycling *(road)*
- ☑ Cycling *(mountain biking)*
- ☑ Outdoor pool
- ☑ Golf
- ☑ Hiking
- ☑ Canoeing
- ☑ Fishing

Facilities: Four good, heated sanitary blocks with free hot water and facilities for babies and disabled visitors. Motorcaravan service point. Laundry with washing machines and dryers. Kitchen with cooking rings, oven and microwave. Small shop at reception. Bar, restaurant and takeaway. Minigolf. Tennis. Fitness trail. Fishing. Canoe hire. Children's club. WiFi (free). Off site: Swimming pool complex adjacent to site (free for campers as is a visit to the zoo). Golf 11 km. Motor racing track at Ring Knutstorp 8 km.

Open: 10 April - 30 September.

Directions: From Malmö: drive towards Lund and follow road no. 108 to Röstånga. From Stockholm: turn off at Østra Ljungby and take road no. 13 to Röstånga. In Röstånga drive through the village on road no. 108 and follow the signs. GPS: 55.996583, 13.28005

Charges guide

Per unit incl. 2 persons
and electricity   € 25,00 - € 33,00

Hafsten SweCamp Resort

Hafsten 120, S-451 96 Uddevalla (Västra Götalands Län)
t: **052 264 4117** e: **info@hafsten.se**
alanrogers.com/SW2725 www.hafsten.se

Accommodation: ☑Pitch ☑Mobile home/chalet ☐ Hotel/B&B ☐Apartment

This privately owned site on the west coast is situated on a peninsula overlooking the magnificent coastline of Bohuslän. Open all year, it is a lovely, peaceful, terraced site with a beautiful, shallow and child friendly sandy beach and many nature trails in the vicinity. There are 190 touring pitches, all with electricity (10A), 100 of them with water and drainage. In all, there are 340 pitches including a tent area and 62 cabins of a high standard. There are plenty of activities available ranging from horse riding at the stables on the campsite's own farm to an 86 m. long water chute. Organised live music evenings with visiting performers are arranged during the summer. Almost any activity can be arranged on the site or elsewhere by the friendly owners if they are given advance notice. Amenities include two clean and well maintained service buildings, a pub, a fully licensed restaurant with wine from their own French vineyard, a well stocked shop and a takeaway. Reception is open and welcoming with natural light used to great effect. This is where the new fitness and wellness facilities can be found.

You might like to know
The site is located between Stromstad, known for its yachting harbour, and Gothenburg, Sweden's second largest city with two universities and the Liseberg amusement park.

- ☑ Riding
- ☑ Tennis
- ☑ Cycling *(road)*
- ☑ Cycling *(mountain biking)*
- ☑ Crafts
- ☑ Sailing
- ☑ Golf
- ☑ Hiking
- ☑ Canoeing
- ☑ Fishing

Facilities: Two heated sanitary buildings provide the usual facilities with showers on payment. Kitchen with good cooking facilities and sinks. Dining room. Laundry facilities. Units for disabled visitors. Motorcaravan services. Shop. Restaurant, takeaway (1/6-31/8) and pub. Live music evenings. TV room. Relaxation centre with sauna and jacuzzi (charged). Well equipped gym. Water slide (charged). WiFi (charged). Riding. Minigolf. Tennis. Boules. Playground. Clay pigeon shooting. Boat hire (canoe, rowing, motor, pedalo). Outside gym/fitness area. Off site: Shopping centre and golf 13 km. Havets hus (marine museum) 30 km. Nordens Ark (animal park) 40 km.

Open: All year.

Directions: From E6, north of Uddevalla, at Torpmotet exit take 161 road towards Lysekil. At Rotviksbro roundabout take 160 road towards Orust. Exit to site is located 2 km. further on left where four flags fly. Follow signs for 4 km. along one-way road for motorcaravans and caravans. GPS: 58.314683, 11.723333

Charges guide

Per pitch incl. electricity	SEK 230 - 355

SWEDEN – Skärholmen

Bredäng Camping Stockholm

Stora Sällskapets väg, S-127 31 Skärholmen (Stockholms Län)
t: **089 770 71**   e: **bredangcamping@telia.com**
alanrogers.com/SW2842   **www.bredangcamping.se**

Accommodation: ☑Pitch ☑Mobile home/chalet   ☐Hotel/B&B   ☐Apartment

Bredäng is a busy city site, with easy access to Stockholm city centre. Large and fairly level, with very little shade, there are 380 pitches, including 115 with hardstanding and 204 with electricity (10A), and a separate area for tents. Reception is open from 08.00-23.00 in the main season (12/6-20/8), reduced hours in low season, and English is spoken. A Stockholm card is available, or a three-day public transport card from the Tube station. Stockholm has many events and activities, you can take a circular tour on a free sightseeing bus, various boat and bus tours, or view the city from the Kaknäs Tower (155 m). The nearest Tube station is five minutes walk; trains run about every ten minutes between 05.00 and 02.00, and the journey takes about twenty minutes. The local shopping centre is five minutes away and a two minute walk through the woods brings you to a very attractive lake and beach.

You might like to know
This site is within easy reach of Stockholm, but also very close to Lake Malaren and just 350 m. from the Mälarhöjdens open-air swimming area.

- ☑ Riding
- ☑ Tennis
- ☑ Cycling *(road)*
- ☑ Crafts
- ☑ Sailing
- ☑ Golf
- ☑ Hiking
- ☑ Canoeing
- ☑ Fishing

Facilities: Four heated sanitary units of a high standard provide British style WCs, controllable hot showers, with some washbasins in cubicles. One has a baby room, a unit for disabled visitors and a first aid room. Cooking facilities are in three units around the site. Laundry facilities. Motorcaravan services and car wash. Well stocked shop, bar, takeaway and fully licensed restaurant (all 1/5-31/8). Sauna. Playground. Off site: Fishing 500 m.

Open: 18 April - 9 October.

Directions: Site is 10 km. southwest of city centre. Turn off E4/E20 at Bredängs signpost and follow clearly marked site signs.
GPS: 59.29560, 17.92315

Charges guide

Per unit incl. electricity	SEK 280 - 325
1-person tent	SEK 120 - 140

Camping Haapasaaren Lomakylä

Haapasaarentie 5, FIN-34600 Ruovesi (Häme)
t: 044 080 0290 e: lomakyla@haapasaari.fi
alanrogers.com/FI2840 www.haapasaari.fi

Accommodation: ☑Pitch ☑Mobile home/chalet ☑Hotel/B&B ☐Apartment

Haapasaaren is located on Lake Näsijärvi, around 70 km. north of Tampere in south western Finland. This is a well equipped site with a café and restaurant, a traditional Finnish outside dancing area and, of course, plenty of saunas! Rowing boats, canoes, cycles and, during the winter months, sleds are all available for rent. Fishing is very popular here. Pitches are grassy and of a good size. There is also a good range of accommodation to rent, including holiday cottages with saunas. The cosy restaurant, Jätkäinkämppä, has an attractive terrace and fine views across the lake. Alternatively, the site's café, Portinpieli, offers a range of snacks as well as Internet access. Haapasaaren's friendly owners organise a series of guided tours throughout the year. These include hiking and nature treks, berry and mushroom picking, and, during the winter, ice fishing and cross-country skiing. Helvetinjärvi National Park is one of the most dramatic areas of western Finland, and is made up of deep gorges and dense forests. There is a rich population of birds and occasionally even brown bears and lynx can be seen here.

Facilities: Café. Restaurant. Direct lake access. Saunas. Fishing. Minigolf. Boat and canoe hire. Bicycle hire. Guided tours. Play area. Tourist information. Chalets for rent. Off site: Walking and cycle routes. Boat trips. Helvetinjärvi National Park.

Open: All year.

Directions: From Helsinki, head north on the E12 motorway to Tampere and then northeast on N63-9 to Orivesi. Then, continue north on route 66 to Ruovesi and follow signs to the site. GPS: 61.99413, 24.069843

Charges guide

Per unit incl. 2 persons and electricity	€ 30,00
extra person	€ 4,50
child (under 15 yrs)	€ 2,00

You might like to know

Some great organised trips are on offer - why not try the berry- and mushroom-picking trips, some cross-country skiing or maybe even ice fishing and burbot catching?

- ☑ Riding
- ☑ Tennis
- ☑ Sports field
- ☑ Hiking
- ☑ Skiing *(cross-country)*
- ☑ Canoeing
- ☑ Fitness/gym
- ☑ Fishing
- ☑ Rowing boats
- ☑ Nordic walking
- ☑ Sled
- ☑ Sauna

FINLAND – Oulu

Nallikari Camping

Leiritie 10, FIN-90510 Oulu (Oulu)
t: **044 703 1353** e: **nallikari.camping@ouka.fi**
alanrogers.com/FI2970 **www.nallikari.fi**

Accommodation: ☑Pitch ☑Mobile home/chalet ☐Hotel/B&B ☐Apartment

This is probably one of the best sites in Scandinavia, set in a recreational wooded area alongside a sandy beach on the banks of the Baltic Sea, with the added bonus of the adjacent Eden Spa complex. Nallikari provides 200 pitches, 176 with 16A electricity (7 also have water supply and drainage), plus an additional 78 cottages to rent, 28 of which are suitable for winter occupation. Oulu is a modern town, about 100 miles south of the Arctic Circle, that enjoys long, sunny and dry summer days. The Baltic however is frozen for many weeks in the winter and then the sun barely rises for two months. In early June the days are very long with the sun setting at about 23.30 and rising at 01.30! Nallikari, to the west of Oulu, is 3 km. along purpose-built cycle paths and the town has much to offer. Nordic walking, with or without roller blades, seems to be a recreational pastime for Finns of all ages! You might even be tempted to buy a pair of long, brightly-coloured walking sticks yourself! Oulu hosts events such as the Meri Oulu Festival in July and the Oulu Music Video Festival and forms the backdrop to the mind boggling, air guitar playing world championships.

You might like to know
Great spa facilities can be found at this site – maybe you could try the Finnish custom of organising a meeting in the sauna facilities!

- ☑ Tennis
- ☑ Cycling *(road)*
- ☑ Golf
- ☑ Hiking
- ☑ Skiing *(downhill)*
- ☑ Aerial walkways
- ☑ Fishing
- ☑ Squash
- ☑ Beach volleyball
- ☑ Minigolf

Facilities: The modern shower/WC blocks also provide male and female saunas, kitchen and launderette facilities. Facilities for disabled visitors. Motorcaravan service point. Playground. Reception with café/restaurant (June-Aug), souvenir and grocery shop. TV room. Free WiFi over site. Bicycle hire. Communal barbecues only. Off site: The adjacent Eden Centre provides excellent modern spa facilities where you can enjoy a day under the glass-roofed pool with its jacuzzis, saunas, Turkish baths and an Irish bath. Riding 2 km. Fishing 5 km. Golf 15 km.

Open: All year.

Directions: Leave road 4/E75 at junction with road 20 and head west down Kiertotie. Site well signed, Nallikari Eden, but continue on, just after traffic lights, cross a bridge and take the second on the right. Just before the Eden Centre turn right towards Leiritie and reception.
GPS: 65.02973, 25.41793

Charges guide

Per unit incl. 2 persons	€ 13,00 - € 26,00
extra person	€ 4,00
child (under 15 yrs)	€ 2,00
electricity	€ 4,50 - € 6,50

Been to any good campsites lately?
We have

You'll find them here...

The UK's market leading independent guides to the best campsites

... also here...

101 great campsites, ideal for your specific hobby, pastime or passion

Want independent campsite reviews at your fingertips?

You'll find them here...

Over 3,000 in-depth campsite reviews at **www.alanrogers.com**

...and even here...

FREE Alan Rogers bookstore app
- digital editions of all 2013 guides
alanrogers.com/digital

An exciting free app from iTunes
the Apple app store or the
Android Market

Want to book your holiday on one of Europe's top campsites?

We can do it for you. No problem.

The best campsites in the most popular regions - we'll take care of everything

alan rogers travel

Discover the best campsites in Europe
with Alan Rogers

alanrogers.com
01580 214000

index

index

index